To Betty Carter and Monica McGoldrick,
brilliant pioneers in the field of family theory and therapy

BY THE AUTHOR

Marriage Rules

The Dance of Fear

The Dance of Connection

The Mother Dance

Life Preservers

The Dance of Deception

The Dance of Intimacy

The Dance of Anger

Women in Therapy

Franny B. Kranny, There's a Bird in Your Hair!
(with Susan Goldhor)

What's So Terrible About Swallowing an Apple Seed?
(with Susan Goldhor)

SunFlower Publishing/Jason Dailey

Harriet Lerner, Ph.D., is one of our nation's most loved and respected relationship experts. A renowned scholar on the psychology of women and family relationships, she is the author of the *New York Times* bestseller *The Dance of Anger* and other acclaimed books, which together have sold more than five million copies. For more than two decades, Lerner served as a staff psychologist at the Menninger Clinic in Topeka, Kansas, and as a faculty member and supervisor in the Karl Menninger School of Psychiatry, and currently is in private practice. Lerner is a distinguished speaker, consultant, and workshop leader who has appeared on *The Oprah Winfrey Show*, CNN, and NPR. She blogs for *The Huffington Post* and hosts *The Dance of Connection* blog on psychologytoday.com. Harriet is also, with her sister, an award-winning children's book writer. She and her husband live in Lawrence, Kansas, and have two grown sons.

www.harrietlerner.com
www.twitter.com/HarrietLerner
www.facebook.com/MarriageRules

MARRIAGE RULES

A Manual for the Married and the Coupled Up

HARRIET LERNER, PH.D.

AVERY

an imprint of Penguin Random House

New York

AVERY

an imprint of Penguin Random House LLC
375 Hudson Street
New York, New York 10014

Previously published in hardcover by Gotham Books
First trade paperback edition, January 2013
Copyright © 2012 by Harriet Lerner

Most Avery books are available at special quantity discounts for bulk purchase for sales promotions, premiums, fund-raising, and educational needs. Special books or book excerpts also can be created to fit specific needs. For details, write SpecialMarkets@penguinrandomhouse.com.

The Library of Congress has catalogued the hardcover edition as follows:

Lerner, Harriet Goldhor.
Marriage rules : a manual for the married and the coupled up / Harriet Lerner.
p.   cm.
ISBN 978-1-59240-691-3
1. Married people—Psychology.   2. Couples—Psychology.
3. Marriage—Psychological aspects.   4. Marital quality.   I. Title.
HQ734.L394   2012   2011032928

ISBN 978-1-59240-745-3 (paperback)

Printed in the United States of America
15   17   19   20   18   16   14

Book design by Spring Hoteling

CONTENTS

AUTHOR'S NOTE
ix

INTRODUCTION
It Shouldn't Be That Complicated
xi

ONE
Warm Things Up
1

TWO
Dial Down the Criticism
23

THREE
Overcome Your L.D.D.
(Listening Deficit Disorder)
47

FOUR
Call Off the Chase:
How to Connect with a Distant Partner
71

FIVE
Fight Fair!
95

SIX
Forget About Normal Sex
119

SEVEN
Kid Shock:
Keep Your Bearings After Children Arrive
149

EIGHT
Know Your Bottom Line
181

NINE
Help Your Marriage Survive Stepkids
209

TEN
Your First Family:
The Royal Road to a Remarkable Marriage
231

EPILOGUE
I Promise You This
259

ACKNOWLEDGMENTS
261

INDEX
265

AUTHOR'S NOTE

This book is inspired by Michael Pollan's slender volume about healthful eating called *Food Rules*, an eater's guide meant to bring much-needed simplicity to our daily decisions about food. "Don't eat breakfast cereals that change the color of the milk," Pollan advises, and "Don't eat anything your great-grandmother wouldn't recognize as food." His rules are all one needs to know to eat wisely and well. Eating, Pollan demonstrates, doesn't have to be so complicated.

Neither does marriage, I thought to myself while thumbing through his book. Why not a book about marriage (defined loosely as couples in a long-term commitment) for those who want just the rules, without the theory behind them? Admittedly, coupling up is more complicated than eating, but I decided it wouldn't be all that difficult to lay out one hundred concise rules that make a relationship work, or at least give it the best chance of succeeding.

I am grateful to Michael Pollan for reminding me that keeping things simple is often the best way to teach the most complicated things.

IT SHOULDN'T BE THAT COMPLICATED

People spend their hard-earned money seeking the advice of relationship experts when they already know what they need to do to have a good marriage—or at least a better one. I was recently reminded of this fact when listening to the marriage vows that two young people said out loud to each other in front of their community of family and friends.

They said in turn:

I promise to always treat you with kindness and respect.

I promise to be faithful, honest, and fair.

I promise to listen carefully to what you are saying.

I promise to apologize when I am wrong and to repair any harm I have done.

I promise to cook and clean for you.

I promise to be your partner and best friend in the best and worst of times.

I promise to bring my best self into our relationship.

I promise to live these promises as a daily practice.

How do you think this couple came up with their shared promises? Did they plow through the countless self-help books and blogs about the "how-tos" of a successful relationship? Did they consult the work of psychologists and marriage counselors and study the latest research on marital failure and success?

Of course not. They consulted their own hearts, their core values, their life experience, and the Golden Rule. By the time we're old enough to choose a life partner, we've observed a number of marriages and have a pretty good idea about what makes things better and worse. We know it's usually a good idea to treat the other person as we'd like to be treated.

If this couple lives their promises as a daily practice (even with a large margin of error), their marriage will do very well, indeed. Need the experts say more?

OK, IT'S NOT THAT SIMPLE

With marriage having a 50 percent no-go rate, it's obvious that people don't follow their promises, or their best thinking, just like people don't eat healthfully even when they know what's good for them. Paradoxically, it's in our most enduring and important relationships that we're least likely to be our most mature and thoughtful selves.

Real life is messy and complicated. When we share a living space with another person, tie our finances together, negotiate sexuality and the countless decisions that daily life demands—well, of course things can go badly. Then there's the baggage we bring from our first family, and all the unresolved issues of the past, to say nothing of all the stresses that pile up as we move along the life cycle. If we make or adopt a baby (never mind adding stepchildren to the picture), it's more difficult still because nothing is harder on a marriage than the addition or subtraction of a family member. In fact, it amazes me that all marriages don't fly apart by the baby's first birthday.

THE FIGHT-OR-FLIGHT RESPONSE

The older I get, the more humble I am about marriage. When anxiety spirals high enough, and lasts long enough, even the most mature relationship may begin to look like a dysfunctional one. To paraphrase the novelist Mary Karr, a dysfunctional marriage is any marriage that has more than one person in it.

I always remind my readers that even the best marriages get stuck in too much distance, too much intensity, and too much pain. Our automatic tendency toward fight or flight is hardwired, and marriage is a lightning rod that absorbs anxiety and intensity from every source. In case you haven't noticed, stress will always be with us.

Life is one thing after another, so it's normal for married folks to yo-yo back and forth between conflict (fight response) and distance (flight response). And just because the universe hands you one gigantic stress, it doesn't mean that it won't hit you with others while you're down. So your mother's health is deteriorating, your dog dies, your son drops out of drug treatment, and your husband is laid off—all in the same year. Unless you are a saint or a highly evolved Zen Buddhist, intimacy with your partner may be the first thing to go.

ARE YOU MOTIVATED TO HAVE A BETTER MARRIAGE?

The rules ahead may look simple, but it is difficult to make a change and especially challenging to maintain it over time. With marriage, as with learning a language or establishing an exercise routine, nothing is more important than motivation.

To put the marriage rules into practice, you'll need to have

1. goodwill and a genuine wish to create a better marriage.

2. an openness to focusing on your self (not self-blame but rather the capacity to observe and change your own steps in a pattern that is bringing you pain).

3. a willingness to engage in bold acts of change.

4. a willingness to practice, practice, practice.

Anything worth doing requires practice, and having a good marriage does too. One can practice choosing happiness over the need to be right or to always win the argument. One can practice playfulness, generosity, and openness. One can practice having both a strong voice and a light touch. One can practice calming things down and warming them up even when the other person is behaving badly. One can practice taking a firm position on things that matter—a position that is not negotiable under relationship pressures.

It helps to know the rules, which you might prefer to think of as pretty good ideas to consider. Sometimes we just need to be reminded of our own common sense. At other times imagination and *un*common sense are required to see an old problem from a new angle. So, take a look at these suggestions and see whether you might be inspired to try something new. It's fine to start small. Small, positive changes have a way of morphing into more generous, expansive ones. Your relationship thanks you in advance.

ONE

WARM THINGS UP

Warm things up? Not everyone responds positively to this suggestion. As one therapy client put it, "I'm supposed to warm her heart and do little things to make her feel special? Give me a break! I've spent most of my life being nice, and I'm not going back there."

He insisted on doing what felt "real and natural," which actually meant doing what was familiar—a life on automatic pilot in a marriage on a downward course.

Sometimes we have to deliberately refrain from criticism and negativity and, instead, experiment with such virtues as kindness and generosity of spirit. This may feel impossible when you're the wronged party and you have a long list of legitimate complaints. Actually, it's not impossible. It's just extremely difficult.

Why should you practice kindness when your partner is behaving badly? The goal is not to put a patina of false brightness over real problems. Rather, kindness, respect, and generosity of spirit prepare the way for authenticity, truth telling, and productive problem solving. As my friend and colleague Marianne Ault-Riché puts it, "It's just when your partner is being the biggest jerk that you're called upon to be your best self."

Rule #1

RESPECT DIFFERENCES!

Marriage requires a profound respect for differences. One of my favorite cartoons, drawn by my friend Jennifer Berman, shows a dog and a cat in bed together.

The dog is looking morose and reading a book called *Dogs Who Love Too Much*.

The cat is saying, "I'm *not* distancing! I'm a cat, damn it!"

I adore this cartoon because marriage goes best when at least one party can lighten up about differences. Of course, we all secretly believe that we have the truth of the universe and that the world would be a better place if everyone were just like us. I have this problem myself. But it is an act of maturity to recognize that differences don't mean that one person is right and the other is wrong.

We all view reality through different filters, depending on our class, culture, gender, birth order, genetic makeup, and unique family history. There are as many views of "the truth" as there are people who hold these views. There are also differences in the habitual ways individuals manage anxiety (under stress, she seeks togetherness, while he seeks distance).

Intimacy requires that we do *not* . . .

(a) *get too nervous about differences.*

(b) *operate as if we have the truth of the universe.*

(c) *equate closeness with sameness.*

"Respecting differences" doesn't mean that we accept demeaning or unfair treatment from our partner. It's just to say that differences don't necessarily mean that one person is right and one person is wrong. Work on staying emotionally connected to a partner who thinks and feels differently than you do without needing to convince or otherwise fix her.

Rule #2
UNDER STRESS, DON'T PRESS

If you're a talker, you may find it hard to live with a more private do-it-yourselfer. Surely this is a difference that makes a difference. Maybe you admired his cool, self-reliant style when you first met, but what initially attracts us and what later becomes "the problem" are often one and the same.

While self-disclosing is one way to be intimate, it's not the only way. Social psychologist Carol Tavris recalls:

> *Years ago, my husband had to have some worrisome medical tests, and the night before he was to go to the hospital we went to dinner with one of his best friends, who was visiting from England. I watched, fascinated, as male stoicism, combined with English reserve, produced a decidedly un-femalelike encounter. They laughed, they told stories, they argued about movies, they reminisced. Neither mentioned the hospital, their worries, or their affection for each other. They didn't need to.*

Try to appreciate the fact that you and your partner may have opposite ways of managing emotional intensity and getting comfortable. You'll do better engaging your partner in conversation if you keep in mind that connection in marriage takes different forms and love is communicated in different ways. Maintaining privacy may not be your partner's way of hiding out but rather his preferred way of being in the world. Try to welcome that "way" rather than wasting energy trying to change it.

Rule #3
BREATHE NOW, SPEAK LATER

Speaking our minds and hearts is at the core of intimacy. We all long to have a marriage that is so relaxed and intimate that we can share anything and everything without thinking about it. Who wants to hide out in a relationship in which we can't allow our self to be known? The dictate "Be Yourself" is a cultural ideal, and luckily no one else is as qualified for the job.

But speaking out and being "honest" are not always good ideas. Sometimes in the name of authenticity and truth telling we shut down lines of communication, diminish and shame the other person, and make it less likely that two people can hear each other or even stay in the same room. We may talk a particular subject to death or focus on the negative in a way that draws us deeper into it.

Make wise and thoughtful decisions about *how* and *when* to say *what* to your partner. You may want to refrain from speaking when you're feeling angry or intense, when your partner is in a bad mood, or when you simply don't have his or her attention.

Timing and tact in marriage are not the opposite of honesty. When emotions are running high, timing and tact are precisely what make honesty possible.

Rule #4
REMEMBER THE 5:1 RATIO

During the courtship stage—or the "Velcro Stage," as I call it—we automatically focus on the positive. We know how to make our partner feel loved and valued and chosen. We may find our differences interesting or exciting, and overlook the negative.

The longer people are coupled up, the more this "selective attention" flips. Now we automatically pay attention to what we are critical about, and *that* is what we notice and speak to. ("Why are you putting so much water in the pot for the pasta?" "Don't you know that's the wrong knife to cut a tomato?") We automatically fail to notice and comment on the positive. ("I loved the way you used humor to deal with your brother on the phone tonight.")

> Aim for a 5:1 ratio of positive to negative interactions.

Try to focus on the positive even if you're feeling angry and resentful. Aim for a 5:1 ratio of positive to negative interactions (marriage expert John Gottman's formula for divorce prevention). If you're feeling very angry with your partner, try the experiment for just one week and see what happens. Even a 2:1 ratio is a good start.

If you can't find much that's positive to speak to in your partner, you've lost perspective. Every individual has some strength and goodness. Every person is better and more complex than the worst things he or she has done. Every relationship has some rewarding elements, even if both partners have forgotten how to notice and comment on them.

Remember that you can communicate interest, generosity, and love in nonverbal ways, as well as with words and language. A simple gesture—a hand on a back, a nod, a smile—can make a person feel seen and cared for.

Rule #5
GOD IS IN THE DETAILS

Many partners do loving and heartwarming things. My husband, Steve, for example, brings me coffee in the morning, usually cooks dinner, and fixes every technological glitch with my computer. He often tells me how much he loves and admires me and how lucky he feels to be married to me. Except on his bad days, he always meets that 5:1 ratio of positive to negative interactions.

But some years back when I was reading Ellen Wachtel's book on couples, *We Love Each Other, But . . .* I realized that Steve had long ago stopped telling me the *specific* things he

> Tell your partner the specific things you admire.

notices and admires, something he did a lot of when we first got together. I also realized that I wasn't making these positive comments to Steve either—not that he was complaining.

Interestingly, adults understand that children of all ages need praise for their specific qualities and behaviors. It's not good enough to say "You're the greatest" and "I love you so much." Kids also need to hear "Great job sharing your toys!" or "I think you were very brave to tell your friend how you felt when she didn't invite you to her birthday party."

At first I felt a little silly even wanting this kind of feedback from Steve. There's a widespread belief that if you have solid self-esteem you don't need affirmation and praise from the outside. (This is patently untrue, by the way.)

I decided to model this behavior myself before asking Steve to make the effort. I experimented for several months with noticing and praising Steve for the specific things I had stopped noticing or simply taken for granted after decades of marriage ("You were so hilarious at the party last night!"). The more I expressed appreciation of Steve's special strengths, the more deeply I appreciated him. Steve did the same for me when I requested it, but I gained the most by being the change I wanted to see.

Rule #6
YOU ALREADY KNOW WHAT TO DO

Books and magazines are filled with tips about how to make a partner feel loved, valued, and special.

You don't need this advice.

No matter how distant your marriage has become, and no matter how dense you claim to be about relationships, you can close this book right now and come up with three specific actions you can take to warm your partner's heart and improve things at home.

> No expert in the universe knows the way you do what warms your partner's heart.

For example, a man I was seeing in therapy insisted he had "tried everything" and was at a total loss about how to improve his marriage. With only the teensiest push, he was able to identify specific actions he knew made his wife feel loved, and he came up with these ideas:

1. I could cook her favorite dish and have dinner ready when she comes home from work tonight.

2. I could organize my stuff in the basement by the end of the month.

3. I could tell her that I want to set up a time to meet Sunday morning to talk about all of her worries

about our daughter Molly. I could just listen and
ask questions for as long as it takes.

No expert in the universe knows the way you do what
warms your partner's heart. It's getting started and sticking
with it that's the hard part.

Rule # 7
REMEMBER THE SANDBOX

There's an old story about two little kids who are play-
ing together in a sandbox with their pails and shovels.
Suddenly a huge fight breaks out and one of the kids
runs away screaming, "I hate you! I hate you!" In no
time at all they're back in the sandbox playing together
happily again.

Two adults observe the interaction from a nearby
bench. "Did you see that?" one asks. "How do children
do that? They were enemies five minutes ago."

"It's simple," the other replies. "They choose happi-
ness over righteousness."

We can save ourselves a great deal of suffering if we strive
to be more like those kids. Folks in long-term relationships
have a terrible time stepping aside from anger and hurt because
our need to be right keeps us from getting back in that sandbox until the other person admits that he started it and is
totally wrong. We lock ourselves into negativity at the expense
of happiness and well-being.

I feel calmed and relieved when my husband, Steve, knocks
at my study door in the middle of a fight, put his arms around
me, and says, "I love you. This is stupid. Let's just drop it."
Many years ago, he invented a silly "1-2-3 let-it-go!" ritual
that makes me laugh and melts my anger. It's a relief when
Steve chooses to be light and playful after we've gone round

and round in a downward spiraling argument, sounding like idiots, even to ourselves.

Obviously there are times when we need to move to the center of a difficult conversation. Some issues need to be revisited, not dropped. We need words to heal betrayals, inequalities, and ruptured connections. But about 85 percent of the time our best bet for relationship happiness is to remember the sandbox—and let those kids be our role model.

Rule #8
FAKE IT FOR TEN DAYS

Perhaps you're thinking you can't abide by any of the rules so far, much less stick to them. You're so angry at your spouse that any sort of "be positive" advice makes you want to gag, especially since it doesn't feel authentic.

Surely no one aspires to be phony or hang out in a relationship where they can't be real. Certainly glib affirmations to "think positively" and "focus on the bright side" can conceal real pain and emotional complexity, inviting us to live a lie, which is more serious than telling one.

But here's the paradox: Couples can get so locked in negativity that sometimes we can only learn what is true, or possible, or "still there" by restraining our so-called true selves. We all need to make a big dent in habitual, unproductive ways of responding to a partner. Experimenting with pretending can be a remarkable achievement in marriage—that is, if you are not pretending out of fear or a wish to deny real problems.

If you're stuck in the negative, consider doing an experiment in creative pretending for ten days. Pretend that your spouse is already the partner that you would like him to be. Pretend appreciation and respect—even joy. This experiment in pretending may help you discover new, more positive truths about you, your partner, and the relationship between you.

Goethe wrote (before inclusive language): "If you treat man as he appears to be, you make him worse than he is. But if you treat man as if he already were what he potentially could be, you make him what he should be." I don't agree that we can make our partner into what he "should be," which probably means what we want him to be. I do know that the person my partner is with me is connected to who I am with him.

Rule #9

SWEAT THE SMALL STUFF

Big issues come in small packages.

When you agree to do something—no matter how small—do it. If you've told her that you'll clean out the refrigerator by Sunday, do it by Sunday. If Sunday comes along and you're too busy, take the initiative to say "I'm really sorry I can't get to it today. I'll do it tomorrow."

Many men tell me they don't understand why their wives get so upset when they "can't remember" to put the cap back on the toothpaste. "I do a thousand things for her," one guy told me. "In fact, I do more than fifty percent. Why does she make such a big deal out of it?"

> When you agree to do something—no matter how small—do it.

Here's the answer: It's a big deal.

When your partner makes a fair request, she needs to know that her voice can affect you. It doesn't matter how trivial the issue is. If you believe that the request is unfair, renegotiate the relationship contract around the "who-does-what" question. ("I know I agreed to take out the garbage Wednesday nights, but that's my biggest workday, and I'd like you to do it.")

Never assume that your overall contribution to a relationship or household compensates for failing to do what you say you'll do. Apologize when you slip up. Do better next time. Don't use your Attention Deficit Disorder (or any other diagnosis, for that matter) as an excuse for irresponsible behavior.

When you say you're going to put the cap on the toothpaste, and then don't, the issue is no longer about a small thing (toothpaste) but a big thing (reliability and respect). Of course you'll slip up. But it's what you do most of the time (not all of the time) that matters.

Rule #10
BE THE ONE TO CHANGE FIRST

If you feel like the "done in" partner, it's natural to want to react in kind. ("Why should I tell him how much I appreciate him when he doesn't appreciate me!")

Why should *you* be the one to change? Surely it's not fair for one person to do all the emotional work in your marriage, or even more than 50 percent.

Here's why:

1. *You are the only person you can change.*

2. *You'll be on more solid ground as a person (whether your marriage improves or not) if you* keep your behavior in line with your core values about how you want to navigate relationships. ("I want to be a person who balances my automatic critical responses with more positive ones.") You'll be on less solid ground if you behave only in reaction to how your partner treats you.

> You are the only person you can change.

3. *If you don't change your part in a stuck pattern, no change will occur.* Change comes from the bottom up—that is, from the person who is in the most pain, or who has the least power, or who

has lost or compromised too much in the relationship. It's the dissatisfied partner who usually is motivated to change. If you don't take some new action on your own behalf, no one else will do it for you.

Remember this: If you want a recipe for relationship failure, just wait for the other person to change first.

TWO

DIAL DOWN THE CRITICISM

A greeting card asks, "If a man is alone in the forest with no woman to criticize him, is he still a schmuck?" Men typically find the card funnier than women do. "That's my experience exactly!" is a common male response. "I can't do anything right. I'm tired of being the target of her nagging and complaining."

It's no surprise that women have a different response. "If those poor guys are so bothered by criticism, why don't they pay attention to it?"

It's common for couples to reach an impasse wherein each person sees the other as the problem and believes that the only "solution" is for their partner to change. He thinks that she has to stop criticizing him and start appreciating all the things that he does for the family. She thinks he has to pay more attention to the needs of the kids and house without her constant reminders. Although the pattern usually breaks down along these gendered lines (distant husband/

nagging wife), it doesn't always. And same-sex couples are not immune to this marital dance.

It's easy to appreciate both perspectives. It feels terrible to be on the receiving end of criticism and just as terrible to be in the role of the "nagging" partner whose legitimate requests are being ignored. When we're feeling angry it's hard to take positive steps to change our part in the pattern because it seems so clear that our partner is the one who should change.

You're lucky if you have a partner who feels so solid, calm, and good about himself that he can let your criticism and negativity slide by him much of the time and consider the good points you are making without distancing or shutting down. But once couples move past the honeymoon or "Velcro" stage of the relationship, such Zen-like forbearance is a rare commodity. Many fine people can't tolerate much criticism or instruction from their partner, even if they truly appreciated it at the early stages of the relationship, when they felt valued and chosen.

If your attempts to reach your partner aren't getting through, it won't help to do more of the same. The habit of criticism is hazardous to any relationship. If you take away just one thing from this book, let it be this: No one can survive a marriage (at least not happily) if they feel more judged than admired.

Rule #11

BECOME FLUENT IN "I" LANGUAGE

The columnist Ellen Goodman once quoted a friend who gave her daughters terrific advice:

> *"Speak up, speak up, speak up!" this mother said. "The only person you'll scare off is your future ex-husband!"*

What an improvement over the prefeminist advice I was raised on: "Listen wide-eyed to his ideas and gracefully add your footnotes from time to time."

All ways of speaking up, however, are not equal. One of the challenges in marriage is to make authentic "I" statements that express your beliefs and feelings without judging or attacking your partner. This may be easy enough if your partner is nodding vigorously in agreement ("I thought you were brilliant tonight") or if the subject matter is a neutral one ("I know you like vanilla, but I prefer chocolate") But when you're dealing with a defensive partner or a high-twitch subject, nothing is simple or easy.

> A true "I" statement is only about you—not your partner.

"I" statements, however, can keep a difficult conversation from exploding into an all-out fight. An "I" statement starts with "I think . . ." "I feel . . ." "I fear . . ." "I want . . ."

Practice making these kinds of statements. And remember that a true "I" statement

- has a light touch.
- is nonjudgmental and nonblaming.
- does not imply that the other person is responsible for your feelings or reactions.
- is only about you—not your partner.

Every "you" statement ("You're being controlling!") can be turned into an "I" statement. ("I need to make my own decision here.") Keep in mind, however, that changing the grammatical structure of your sentences is only part of the challenge. You also need to get the edge out of your voice. An intense, reactive tone will "undo" even the most carefully constructed "I" statement and may come across as blaming. So hold off until you can state your "I" position calmly. Practice this too!

Rule # 12

BEWARE OF PSEUDO "I" LANGUAGE!

We may think we're talking in "I" language when we stick "I think" or "I feel" in front of a sentence. This doesn't do the trick, because true "I" language must meet the four criteria in the previous rule.

Sometimes it's easy to detect a *pseudo* "I" statement ("I think you have a narcissistic personality disorder") that judges or diagnoses the other person. In many cases, however, the difference between a *true* "I" statement and a *pseudo* "I" statement can be subtle, as the following two examples illustrate.

A TRUE "I" STATEMENT

Alice, a psychology colleague, tells this story of her productive shift into "I" language.

> My husband, Ken, and I were recently driving home from a party. Our kids were asleep in the backseat. It was raining fairly heavily, and I felt Ken was driving too fast, given the weather.
>
> "You're speeding," I said.
>
> "I'm going under the speed limit," he responded.
>
> "You're driving recklessly for this weather—and with your kids in the backseat," I exclaimed.
>
> This made Ken really angry. "You're accusing me of endangering our children? I've never been in an accident, and I'm going under the speed limit."

I shifted gears. "What I really mean is just that I'm uncomfortable driving at this speed, rightly or wrongly. Would you please slow down, even if I'm overreacting?"

"Of course," Ken said and slowed down without further argument.

In switching from accusations to an "I" statement, Alice gave Ken the space to slow down without feeling he was admitting to being a reckless father and driver. Alice would be the first to admit he's neither.

A PSEUDO "I" STATEMENT

This story, told by a friend about his wife, Jill, illustrates an "I" statement that was really a "you" statement dressed up in "I" statement clothing.

My home office has been a mess lately, and Jill, who shares the space, is a much more organized person than I am. After glancing at the stacks of papers everywhere on my desk and floor, she said to me,

"When I walk into this room, I feel like our household is totally falling apart."

Totally falling apart! Our household? I'm her hardworking, faithful partner of fourteen years, and because my half of the office is a mess she feels like everything is crumbling around her? And yet when I said, "That's a pretty extreme statement," she simply responded, "Well, it's how I feel."

How can I possibly respond to that?

A partner is unlikely to have the space to consider his behavior, much less apologize for it, if he feels he's putting his head on the chopping block and taking responsibility for not only his behavior but for your unhappiness as well. An "I" statement should serve to clarify your position, not act as a Trojan horse for smuggling in judgments and accusations.

Rule #13
CRITICIZE ABOVE THE BELT

When we're angry about not being heard, we may automatically resort to any number of below-the-belt tactics. We leap from the facts ("You said you'd clean up the kitchen and I need you to do it") to a damning generalization ("When you say you'll do something, I can never count on you to follow through"). Perhaps we throw in a label ("I can't believe how insensitive you are") along with a diagnosis ("You have a narcissistic personality") and bring in another party or two to bolster our case ("My therapist thinks that you're passive aggressive, and my sister agrees"). While we're at it, we may slip in an interpretation along the way ("You may think I'm your mother, but I'm not here to serve you like she did") and remind him that he needs therapy. And we serve all of this up in a condescending, mocking, preaching, and blaming tone.

> Constructive criticism focuses on actions, not character judgments.

Wonder of wonders that our partners don't seem to appreciate our feedback.

Constructive criticism, by contrast, asks for a specific behavioral adjustment that honors your partner's capacity to change. It focuses on actions, not character judgments. The "lightly served" part is especially important if your partner responds poorly to anger or intensity in your voice. People can say very difficult things if they calmly present the facts with no edge in their voice. Silliness helps enormously, as when my son's wife threatened to charge him rent if he kept putting his clothes on her desk.

A constructive complaint looks like this: You calmly ask him not to leave his things flung around the house, not because he's a big slob (although that may be so) but because neatness is important to you. You "own" the problem ("I'm just not comfortable when you leave your briefcase and coat on the living room couch") and appreciate that there are other women in the world who would be happy living with someone who didn't pick up after himself. You mention the attacks you made earlier, at a time of frustration, and you apologize for them.

At a relaxed time, you invite a conversation ("Can we make a rule about where briefcases and coats are kept?") and figure out how to compromise on your different styles. You appreciate that change occurs slowly, in fits and starts, so you praise him for moves in the right direction. After all, you couldn't transform yourself into a person comfortable with clutter overnight. You might even conclude that it would be simpler to sweep through the house twice a day and dump all his belongings on his big armchair until he decides what to do with them, if anything.

After studying thousands of married couples, marriage expert John Gottman concluded that criticism (the nonconstructive kind) is one of "the four horsemen of the apocalypse," which can clip-clop into the heart of a marriage and can destroy it. For anyone who has that intention, Gottman suggests adding the gibe "What's wrong with you?"

Rule #14
AIM FOR ACCURACY

When you have a specific complaint, aim for accuracy. Anyone who is criticized inaccurately may hear only the exaggerations and inaccuracies and become unable to consider the valid point being made.

Don't overstate your point. Avoid globalizing words like "always" and "never." If your husband came home late from work six times last month, don't exaggerate the number. People on the receiving end of criticism shut down on the spot if they catch an error or believe that they are being held responsible for more than their fair share of the problem. I recall any number of stupid fights with my husband when I flatly refused to apologize because he was blaming me for 75 percent of the problem and I was convinced I was only, um, maybe 52 percent to blame.

Rule #15
TALK LESS

Over-talking on your part will lead to under-listening from your partner (and vice versa). People take in very little information when they don't want to hear what you're saying. If you go on too long, you're actually protecting your partner, because he may shut down and vacate the emotional premises. He won't have the space to sit with what you've said and to consider the valid point you may be making.

Keep in mind that less is more. When people feel they can't get through, they often lengthen their arguments or raise their voices. This does not help—and usually hurts. And we may not recognize that the sheer number of sentences may be the culprit.

Practice saying difficult things in three sentences, making your point only once in a particular conversation. Slow down your speech and turn down the volume. Try this for ten days. I confess that this is an especially difficult challenge for me, particularly the three-sentence limit. My automatic tendency is to amplify my case if my husband doesn't immediately grasp the "truth" as I see it.

> Making your point in three sentences or fewer gives your partner the space to consider it.

Don't think in terms of "getting results" ("He still doesn't listen!"). Rather, stay focused on the experiment of modifying your own style. It can be incredibly difficult to say *only* "I want you to say 'thank you' when I cook you dinner," or "You forgot to take the garbage out for the second week in a row," or "I feel uncomfortable about how much you drank at the party," and leave it at that.

Making your point in three sentences or fewer gives your partner the space to consider it. Obviously, longer conversations are necessary on many subjects. But these conversations will go better if you practice brevity on a daily basis.

Rule #16
STRIKE WHEN THE IRON IS COLD

Sometimes a show of real fury will get your partner's attention, especially if blowups are the exception, not the rule, and disconnections get quickly repaired. But often the worst time to speak is when you're feeling angry and intense.

Save your criticism until both of you have calmed down and you're feeling good about your partner. But don't save it for a special occasion, such as his birthday, when you've finally gotten a sitter and you're going out to dinner at a restaurant for the first time in a month! Simply pick a time when the emotional climate between you is relaxed and you have his attention.

Being human, you're not always going to save your complaints for better weather. If your partner walks in an hour late for dinner because he stopped off at the electronics shop to buy something for his iPod, of course you're going to tell him, without false sweetness, that the dinner is cold, the kids are driving you crazy, and you need him to come straight home from work or call if he can't.

In the heat of the moment try to follow the three-sentence rule and leave it at that. Simply venting anger and criticism won't change a pattern, such as chronic lateness, from which your anger springs. At a different time, when you actually like him, ask him if there's a time the two of you can meet for twenty minutes to figure out a solution to the problem at hand. Requesting a brief meeting works better than the dreaded "We have to talk!" line, which typically raises a partner's anxiety and fuels your own self-righteousness. A judicious "time-out" can prevent many a marital meltdown.

Rule # 17
STAY FOCUSED

When you sit down to discuss a complaint, stick to one criticism per discussion. ("You bought the TV before we could talk about the size and color. We had agreed that we wouldn't make major purchases without the other person's full input.") Don't tag on past infractions even when it's relevant. ("Last year you purchased that truck without even considering whether we could afford it, and I'm still mad about that.") Avoid getting into side issues. ("You said you'd work on your overspending, and now you bounced two checks!")

Staying focused also means not getting sidetracked by your partner's counterpunches. If he comes back with an item from your crime sheet ("How can you complain about the TV when you just loaned your brother five hundred dollars?"), let him know you'd be glad to address his concern in a different conversation, but now you want to focus on the issue of sharing decisions on major purchases. If the conversation starts going downhill, set up another time to revisit the issue.

"Stay focused" may sound like one of the simpler rules. It's not. Both in love and work it requires considerable motivation, self-observation, and practice to keep a conversation focused on one issue at a time, with an eye toward creative problem solving.

Rule #18
SURPRISE HIM WITH PRAISE

Get off automatic pilot and surprise your partner with a compliment at the very moment he's expecting to hear the same old criticism.

Ellen disliked being with Bob's family because her husband always got into the same political argument with his father. Bob's participation in these verbal duels accomplished nothing except adding to the tension and unpleasantness of the visit. Countless times, Ellen had given her husband wise advice about how to lighten things up when his dad got provocative.

Bob consistently ignored her good advice, or perhaps he couldn't make use of it. He kept getting into it with his dad. On the car rides home, Ellen would unleash a barrage of advice and criticism. She recognized that Bob wasn't altering his part in the same old dance with his dad, but she couldn't see that she was doing the same with her husband.

At my suggestion, Ellen decided to surprise Bob by substituting praise for criticism. After the next visit, they started the drive home in silence. Then, after lightly joking that Bob's father was a piece of work, Ellen said thoughtfully, "You know, Bob, I admire you so much for hanging in with your family. No matter how difficult it gets, you keep showing up."

"Why are you being so nice?" Bob snapped back. Ignoring his tone, Ellen said warmly, "I realize I have to figure out how to have more of a relationship with my parents rather than being the expert on your family. And that insight made me realize how much I admire your commitment to your dad and mom. It's the lesson I'd want to teach our kids when we have them—that even when family members are really difficult, you still show up."

Try this experiment in your own marriage. If your partner expects criticism, astonish him instead with sincere praise. Avoiding a predictable pattern of criticism will give him more space to consider the merits of the suggestions you've already made. An authentic compliment boosts the likelihood that you and your partner can discuss the issue in fresh ways in the future.

Rule #19
TAKE THE "ONE-A-DAY" CHALLENGE

One criticism a day! Who am I kidding? I had seven criticisms today just from one of Steve's grocery shopping expeditions. Of course, I believed that every comment was crucial to his shopping education. Luckily, he was in a good mood and simply agreed with most of what I said and let the rest float by him.

Steve is generally easygoing, but when he's not, our relationship could definitely benefit from the "one-a-day" rule. This rule is especially important for those of us who reflexively criticize or instruct our partner as a habitual way of responding when we're under stress—which may be a great deal of the time, even if we're not aware of it. If we practice limiting ourselves to one criticism a day, we will think more clearly about what really matters in our marriage and let the rest go.

My best "Let the rest go" lesson was a vacation Steve and I took to Mexico some years back. On this trip we agreed that we would not speak one word of English—not to each other or anybody else. Because I was equipped with a very small Spanish vocabulary, I had to learn to settle into silence, because even a simple comment to Steve would have required me to consult the dictionary. Obviously, I lacked the grammar for elegant complaints such as "If you had only been thoughtful enough to let me know how late you'd be, I would have preferred to meet you at the cathedral."

Realistically, I can't suggest that you and your partner

forgo your native tongue for a while so you can experience
how many of your criticisms—to say nothing of your good
advice—can go by the wayside. Just take my word for it: One
criticism a day is sufficient. Figuring out which one matters
most is a good exercise. Start with just the weekends, and see
how you do.

Rule #20

CUT BACK ON ADVICE

Critical? *Moi?*

Often we don't see ourselves as critical because we're trying to be helpful by explaining how to do things correctly. We know we're right, and we well might be, whether it's about a small thing (how to fold the towels) or a big thing (how to balance next year's budget).

So, what's wrong with advice giving, especially if we're right? Nothing is wrong if the other person asks for advice. Nothing is wrong if there is balance in the relationship between giving and receiving counsel. Many couples give endless unsolicited advice to each other with no problem and value the opportunity to learn from each other.

But advice giving is problematic when it kicks the relationship out of balance or if one partner is better at giving, rather than receiving, advice. It shades into criticism when there are too many little corrections, or we deliver it in an "I know what's best" tone. And if the other person doesn't follow our advice, it's a good indication that we shouldn't be giving it.

If you're a firstborn sibling with a younger, same-sex sibling, you may be especially prone to wanting your partner to do things the right way, which is your way. If your partner truly values such guidance, there's no problem. If he doesn't value it, it's his responsibility to make himself heard and tell you to back off.

The problem is that he may not be a clear communicator. He may not even be aware of how much easier the relationship would feel if you did less steering. It might surprise him to discover that he feels more relaxed and competent when you're out of town for a week or two.

What matters in a relationship is not that things get done according to who is right. What matters is that two people are dedicated to contributing to each other's happiness. That includes giving each other the space to make mistakes and develop competence through trial and error, and being available to help—when asked.

Rule #21

STAY ALERT FOR MIXED MESSAGES

Rather than clearly telling you to back off, your partner may give you mixed messages. "Mixed message" communication is common and, apart from being indecipherable, it runs the risk of encouraging us to miss feedback from our partner. Consider the following conversation that occurred in my office:

She: Do you think I'm bossy?

He: Well, yes. You're definitely bossy. We've talked about that.

She: Was I bossy last night?

He: Like when I was cutting tomatoes for the salad, you said, "Why are you cutting them that way?" Then you said the pieces were too small and it's better to slice them in even pieces. And I think there's too much of that. I mean you do it a lot.

She: A lot? What do you mean?

He: Well, you do it with other people too. Remember what happened at my brother's house on Thanksgiving when his wife got mad at you and said, "This is my house and would you please let me do things my way."

She: But I was only trying to be helpful. I was right that she didn't make enough potatoes, and the turkey wasn't done on time.

He: I know. My brother's wife is a difficult person. You really did save the turkey.

*She: And with the tomatoes last night, you yourself said they
looked better sliced in even pieces.*

*He: Well, yeah, I guess you're really the expert in the kitchen,
so maybe it's a good thing.*

If you get a mixed message like this one, ignore the
"maybe it's a good thing" part. Back off and give him space
to cut the tomatoes (and whatever else) his own way, unless
he's your sous-chef for the evening, in which case the contract is to follow your orders. Sure you should say something
if he's put on a stained shirt for an important meeting or he's
about to set the house on fire. But most of what you feel
compelled to correct doesn't matter as much as you think.

THREE

OVERCOME YOUR L.D.D.
(Listening Deficit Disorder)

How we talk and listen to each other defines how our marriage goes and whether or not we are happy to see our partner at the end of the day. It comes as no surprise that most of us are more motivated to improve our talking skills than to attend to the other half of the conversational equation. When differences arise, our wish to be heard and understood is naturally greater than our wish to hear and understand our partner.

We may believe that what we say, and how we say it, has a greater influence on our partner than how we listen. In fact, improving how we listen is fundamental to knowing our partner and being known, resolving conflict, and improving the chances that our partner will listen more openly to what we have to say.

You may observe that you're a better listener with a friend or a coworker than you are with your partner. This is not necessarily a problem. The nice thing about marriage is that two people can make do with giving each other their distracted and partial attention a great deal of the time, and still have a good relationship. When something is important, however, you need to shift out of a distracted or defensive mode and bring a different quality of emotional presence to the table.

I was taught in a graduate school class that listening is a passive process, but this is not so. Listening is an active process, and one that comes less naturally than talking. A good listener does more than sit there and make empathic grunts. True listening requires you to quiet your mind, open your heart, and ask questions to better understand what your partner is saying. It also requires you to stop yourself from interrupting and saying things that leave your partner feeling unheard or cut short. It requires you to get past your defensiveness when your partner is saying things that challenge your favored image of yourself so that her voice and her pain can affect and influence us. And it's important to let your partner know when you're not in a position to listen fully—to know when to say to your partner "Not now" or "Not in this way."

Listening with an open heart is the ultimate spiritual act. It is one of the greatest gifts you can give to your partner, and ultimately to yourself. Intimacy with your partner rises or falls in direct proportion to your capacity to listen well. Here are the rules for doing that.

Rule #22

DON'T JUST DO SOMETHING. STAND THERE!

A common problem I hear from couples goes like this: One person says, for example, "I'm feeling X" and the other immediately says, "Have you considered doing Y or Z?" rather than letting the conversation unfold without a solution.

Getting "solution focused" before our partner has asked for our help reflects a wish to be helpful that isn't helpful at all. Advice giving blocks listening and can leave our partner feeling unheard and isolated in the relationship. Part of the problem is that we confuse our partner's sharing a problem with inviting us to take over. Or we may feel that we have to resolve a problem in a single conversation, rather than recognizing that we can have several conversations over time.

The next time you want to move in quickly to offer a solution, tell yourself, "This is conversation *number one*. I'm not going to offer any advice until conversation number two, which I can initiate later." Your advice is most likely to be helpful if you listen first. And learning to be a caring listener and a skilled questioner can go a long way toward empowering your partner to find his own solutions.

Rule #23

STAY CURIOUS: YOU DON'T REALLY
KNOW HOW SHE FEELS!

A common type of misguided empathy is telling your partner that you know just how she or he feels. The desire to
"totally relate" to what another person is going through arises
from good intentions, but it denies the depth and complexity
of your partner's situation and can turn the attention back to
yourself. ("I know just how you feel because I remember how
scared I was before my gallbladder surgery.")

I've frequently observed the problem of the listener
eclipsing the other's experience, and it leaves the person who
is trying to tell her story feeling abandoned. We want others
to honor the specificity of our story, not simply identify it
with his own.

When our friends Stephanie and James had dinner with
us recently, Stephanie shared her experience of depression—
something she'd struggled with on and off, but never as
intensely as in the past week. She said that even simple tasks,
like eating breakfast and paying the electric bill, were beginning to feel almost impossible. James, a wonderful husband
who is blessed with an upbeat disposition, kept following
Stephanie's descriptions of her worsening depression with
statements like "I know just what you mean. Sometimes I just
don't want to get out of bed and go to work."

James's intentions were good—he wanted to make Stephanie feel understood, and to make her experiences seem

"normal." But James, who had never dealt with anything like a clinical depression, was in fact failing to hear the experiences Stephanie was courageously sharing.

At one point Erica, another friend at the dinner table, said to Stephanie, "I've never had to go through what you're describing, and it sounds profoundly difficult. I'm really impressed that you have the courage to be so open about it. Is there anything we can do to be helpful?" Both James and Erica wanted Stephanie to feel supported. But Erica's statement honored the different and specific nature of Stephanie's experience, whereas James's comments equated Stephanie's struggle with his occasional grumpy mornings.

James, to his credit, was able to observe how his attempts to "relate" had minimized what Stephanie was going through. He also realized that he'd been afraid to hear how terrible she felt. As the conversation unfolded, he began to understand the seriousness of Stephanie's depression and about the need to seek help if it persisted.

Staying deeply curious about your partner's experience *without* identifying it with your own story is a crucial and undervalued part of listening. Honoring your partner's difference instead of reducing it to sameness allows for a much deeper connection.

In fact, we can never truly know another person's experience. Try saying "I can't imagine what you're going through," or "It sounds excruciating," or "I'm so sorry you're having to deal with this, and I want you to know I'm here for you."

Rule #24
FORGET ABOUT BEING RIGHT

We can't listen well when our mind is already made up and we have our own agenda. Instead of trying to understand what our partner is saying, we're likely to be waiting for him to finish talking so we can launch into our own argument.

Being right is often beside the point. There is no simple "right" answer to decisions we make as couples, and fostering a collaborative spirit instead of a competitive debate is more important than defending any particular position.

Bob and his wife engaged in repetitive, downward-spiraling fights about whether they should stay in their large house (as she wanted) or downsize (as he insisted). Both could recognize that "here we go again" feeling whenever this issue arose, but nothing changed until Bob took the initiative to change his part of the pattern.

During a couples session in my office, Bob suddenly stopped arguing and instead asked questions to better understand the viewpoint of his wife, Laura. He intentionally shifted into a place of pure listening, detaching from the question of who was correct or what was true and how he could best make his case. Who knew why? Perhaps he was inspired by a new creative project he had just started, which bolstered his sense of self-worth and allowed him to be more emotionally generous.

Bob's automatic tendency was to get stuck on correcting facts—for example, when Laura made incorrect statements about the house payments or mortgage. Now he resisted getting sidetracked by details and instead made an effort to stay "on point" about his wife's strong wish to stay in their house. When she put him down ("The house doesn't matter to you because you're always at the office"), he initially got defensive ("I'm not ALWAYS in the office—and if I *weren't* in the office, we wouldn't have the house"). He recovered quickly, however, and changed direction. He looked at Laura and said, "It's true. You've put so much more of yourself into the house than I have. You're there more, and you've really made it beautiful."

Laura visibly softened. She shared her vulnerability, recalling that she had made endless moves as a child and never knew where home would be for long. By the end of the session, they weren't so polarized. In fact, they had a plan. Laura would drive around with Bob on Saturdays to see what smaller places were available and at what price—not because she agreed to move but just as part of a fact-gathering expedition. They would also look at their finances together and crunch the numbers to see whether they could stay in the big house "forever." Bob would work harder to appreciate how much the old house meant to Laura, and to factor her love for their home into the staying-or-leaving equation. They each left the session feeling more like partners than adversaries.

> Try to catch yourself when your focus on being right prevents you from working toward a common purpose.

Try to catch yourself when your focus on being right prevents you from working toward a common purpose. Moving from defensiveness to genuine curiosity about your partner's position is more important than scoring points in an argument. Ask questions lovingly, because if your questions are delivered in an intense manner, your partner may feel like you're cross-examining her rather than trying to know her better.

Rule #25
INVITE WHAT YOU DREAD

If you're sick of hearing your partner's repetitive worry or complaint about a particular subject, challenge yourself and surprise her by inviting the very conversation you most dread.

You might think that you'll be opening the floodgates by asking your partner about something she's already overfocused on, whether it's your unavailability after dinner or her worry about your son's bad grades. In fact, the opposite is true. She will feel less intense and thus less obsessed if you *invite* her to tell you everything and you are fully present to hear it.

What does this "ultimate listening experiment" look like?

A while ago, I was having a hard time with both the health and appearance aspects of aging, having accumulated what I felt was more than my fair share. Steve tired of hearing the same thing over and over, and his attention span shrank. He'd say things like "You keep going over and over the same thing. It's not helping you, and there's nothing you can do about it anyway." Or he'd point out how much I had to be grateful for, how far worse off others were, how someday a truly terrible thing would happen to me or him or someone in the family, so why was I wasting the good time I had now.

All true of course. But I'm allergic to the message "It is what it is, it can't be fixed, so let's move on." Nor is it generally a good idea in marriage to rule a subject off-limits, at least not permanently. Men often tell me, "I'm not going to ask her about *that*!"—*that* being the criticism they can't stand hearing or the worry they feel their partner is blowing out of proportion. They don't realize that if their partner feels muzzled, or not truly heard, she'll become more obsessed.

I don't know what inspired Steve, but one evening he said, "I want us to have a glass of wine in the living room after dinner, and I want you to tell me all about the changes you're going through physically and how you feel about them. I want to hear every single detail, and I just want to listen." He suggested I start with the top of my head down to the bottom of my feet and tell him *everything*. He listened with great care and asked questions to elicit more details. He made no move to end the conversation. When I finally stopped talking, he asked, "Is there more you haven't told me?"

What Steve *didn't* do was as important as what he did. He didn't interrupt or offer advice, wisdom, reassurance, or messages of good cheer. He didn't criticize, judge, or minimize my experience ("I think you're overreacting"). He didn't answer or check his phone.

Try this ultimate listening experiment with your partner. Set up a meeting time to listen when you're free of distraction and have good intentions. Consider where to talk. The bedroom or kitchen may not be as relaxing as talking in the living room or an outdoor setting. Let your partner know in advance that you are there to learn everything about what she's upset or angry about. Ask her if you really "got it."

Rule #26
DRAW THE LINE AT INSULTS!

I tend to be ill-tempered and obnoxious every now and then, although I try not to make a habit out of it. When Steve is in a light mood, he lets my bad behavior float by him, or he responds with humor and silliness.

He also has no problem saying "I'm not continuing this conversation until you can talk to me in a different tone of voice and with respect." Depending on his mood, Steve can stop a conversation with great maturity or great immaturity. Either way, he's clear about what sort of exchanges he won't participate in. He'll end a conversation right then and there if I continue to approach him as if he were a big screwup rather than a collaborative partner.

Don't continue a conversation that is at your expense, especially if this has become a pattern in your marriage rather than an occasional occurrence. Crying, pleading, or trying to reason with someone who isn't listening or showing respect will only lead to a downward spiral. You need to walk away.

When you exit from one conversation (which may mean leaving the room or the house), you can offer the possibility of another. ("I want to hear what bothers you, but I want you to approach me differently. Let's try again later when we're both calmer.")

Listening to your partner with an open heart is not the same as allowing yourself to be demeaned or badly treated.

Rule #27
LOWER YOUR DEFENSIVENESS: A 12-STEP PROGRAM

We're all defensive a fair amount of the time, although we may be better able to observe defensiveness in *other* people. Just a little bit of anxiety is enough to reduce the listening part of the human brain to the size of a pinto bean.

> Defensiveness is normal and universal. It is also the archenemy of listening.

Once we're in defensive or reactive mode we can't take in new information or see two sides of an issue—or better yet, seven or eight sides. Defensiveness is normal and universal. It is also the archenemy of listening.

Here are twelve steps that can help us lower our defensiveness.

1. *Name it.* Defensiveness is that immediate, knee-jerk "But, but . . . But . . ." response and heightened sense of tension that may be activated when our partner says, "We have to talk." In defensive mode, we *automatically* listen for the inaccuracies, exaggerations, and distortions in our partner's complaint so that we can refute errors, make our case, and remind the other party of *their* wrongdoings. Becoming aware of our

defensiveness can give us a tiny, crucial bit of distance from it.

2. *Breathe.* Defensiveness starts in the body. When we feel threatened, our central nervous system overheats and makes us tense and on guard, unable to take in much new information. So, do what you can to calm yourself. Try slowing down your breathing, exhaling to a slow, silent count of one to ten, and taking a long, deep breath between the time your partner's voice drops off and yours starts. We will always listen poorly when we're tense and on guard with an overheated central nervous system.

3. *Don't interrupt.* If you can't listen without interrupting, it's a good indication that you haven't calmed down. Trying to listen when you can't does more harm than good. Tell your partner that you want to have the conversation, and that you recognize its importance, but that you can't have it right now.

4. *Ask for specifics.* This will help clarify your partner's point and show that you care about understanding her. ("Can you give me another example where you felt I was putting you down?") Note: Asking for specifics is not the same thing as nitpicking—the key is to be curious, not to

cross-examine. Don't act like a lawyer even if
you are one.

5. *Find something to agree with.* You may only agree
    with 2 percent of what your partner is saying
    but still find a point of commonality in that
    2 percent ("I think you're right that I've been
    coming home stressed-out from work"). This
    will shift the exchange out of combat into col-
    laboration.

6. *Apologize for your part.* There's almost always
    something to apologize for when we've had a
    difficult experience with a partner. Even making
    a general and genuine comment like "I'm sorry
    for my part in all of this" can indicate to your
    partner that you're capable of taking responsibil-
    ity, not just evading it.

7. *No buts.* When we're defensive, we may begin a
    slew of sentences with "But"—re*but*ting what we
    should be trying to take in. Even if we're listen-
    ing with open minds, the word *"but"* conveys the
    impression that we are discounting or negating
    the other person's perspective. Watch out for
    this little grammatical sign of defensiveness and
    temporarily ban it from your vocabulary. Instead,
    ask "Do I have this right?" and "Is there more
    you haven't told me?"

8. *Don't countercriticize.* There is a time to bring up your own grievances, but that time is not when your partner has taken the initiative to voice her complaints. If your complaints are legitimate, all the more reason to save them for a time when they can be a focus of conversation and not a defense strategy.

9. *Let your partner know he or she has been heard.* Even if nothing has been resolved, tell your partner that she's reached you: "It's not easy to hear what you're telling me, but I want you to know that I'm going to give it a lot of thought." Take a day to genuinely consider her point of view.

10. *Sit with your response.* When we're feeling defensive, we try to do everything in one conversation, as if it's the last one we're ever going to have. Tell yourself early on that you're going to take a day to think about your partner's point of view and that you don't have to make all your points now. If you decide this in advance, it will free you to listen better and help your partner feel heard.

11. *Try thanking your partner for initiating the talk.* Even if you don't like what your partner is saying, you can thank her for initiating a difficult conversation. Relationships require that we take such initiative and express gratitude when our

partner might expect mere defensiveness. In this way we can calm things down and signal our commitment to open communication.

12. *Bring the conversation up in the next forty-eight hours.* Show your partner that you are continuing to think about her point of view and that you are willing to revisit the issue. Try saying something like "I've been thinking about our conversation, and I'm really glad that we had that talk."

Listening without defensiveness is a challenge of a lifetime. Begin with the first three steps (Name it, Breathe, Don't interrupt) and give yourself a medal of honor if you achieve just that.

Rule #28
DEFINE YOUR DIFFERENCES

Listening well to criticism does not mean that you're an overly accommodating, peace-at-any-price kind of person who doesn't speak up. A joke among men maintains that the husband should always have the last word in any confrontation—and that the last word should be "You're right, honey. I'm wrong. I'm really sorry and I'll never do it again."

After you have truly listened and considered your partner's point of view, you need to tell her how you see things differently. For instance, you might say "I thought about our conversation, and I'm really sorry I ignored you at the party. But I don't agree that I made you drink too much. I'm responsible for my behavior, but I'm not responsible for yours."

Defining your differences (and allowing your partner to do the same) is at the heart of having both a self and a relationship. Remember that a critical partner will listen better to your different point of view if you save it for a future conversation, or at least until after your partner feels fully heard and understood. Even if your partner isn't able to consider your point of view, you need to hear the sound of your own voice saying what you really think.

Rule #29
HELP YOUR PARTNER HELP YOU LISTEN

Don't give up on your partner, who may have a style you find so critical, intense, or difficult that you've shut down. Instead, tell her what you need in order to listen and stay in the conversation. Keep telling her for as long as it takes.

A man I saw in therapy was married to a woman who over-talked things in a rapid-fire way when she was anxious, which was most of the time. Over the years he began to distance and stonewall, which only raised her anxiety and intensified her rat-a-tat-tat style.

> Tell your partner what you need in order to listen. Keep telling her for as long as it takes.

He made a big move forward when he approached her at a calm time and said warmly, "Honey, I want to listen to you better. I think because of experiences growing up in my family, I'm allergic to conflict and intensity. When you start off with a list of criticisms or you share your worries in such an intense way, I feel flooded and I withdraw. I'm trying to work on my problem in therapy, and I've also been thinking of ways you can help me to be a better partner."

He then asked her to try to approach him calmly—that is, with slower speech, lower volume, and less urgency. He asked her to please bring up one criticism at a time. He also said, "It's hard for me to listen to your worries about the kids when I've just walked in the door or we're sitting down to dinner. I prefer we plan a time to talk about what's bothering you and give it all the time you need."

He explained that his wish was not to control her but rather to share how easily he felt flooded and agitated in the face of intensity. He owned the problem without blaming her for his feelings. He spoke to the positive by saying, "I know that what I react to is the other side of what I love about you—your energy and vitality, and how openly you address things."

Obviously, his wife couldn't modulate her intensity overnight any more than he could stay calm and in good humor when she was in pursuit mode. He continued to end conversations that ranked too high on his intensity meter, and to resume them at a calmer time.

Still, he helped her understand that he was not just a passive-aggressive guy trying to avoid all difficult conversation. You'll be a better listener if you can help your partner understand what's getting in the way of your listening better without criticizing or blaming her for the problem.

Rule #30
SET LIMITS ON LISTENING

We all have our limits on how much we can listen, just as we have limits on how much we can give or do. When your capacity to listen has been exceeded, you need to find a way to end the conversation or creatively steer it in a different direction. There is nothing compassionate about letting a person go on after you've shut down. Nor is it compassionate only to listen and never share your own problems or pain.

Jim, a therapy client of mine, reported that his wife Sarah was relentlessly focused on the poor care her dad was receiving at a nursing home. She would bring it up almost every evening, typically over dinner. Jim started to dread the conversation. Eventually he tuned it out, because he felt that limiting the conversation would be insensitive and that Sarah would bring it up anyway, despite his protests.

I worked with Jim on figuring out how to approach Sarah about the situation and interrupt the pattern. Over time he learned to gently interrupt Sarah when she began to talk about her father. He would say things like the following:

Sarah, I know how upset you are about the poor treatment your dad is getting. But sometimes I feel as if I'm losing my precious time with you because it's taking up so much of our evenings. I'm having a hard time at work right now, and I want to talk to you about that.

Sarah, I'm committed totally to being there for you around this problem, but I don't want us to have this conversation during our cooking and dinner time, and I can't really give it my best attention when I want to relax. Let's have coffee this weekend and talk about your dad.

And (in a light, warm, and teasing way), Sarah, if you mention that nursing home one more time during dinner tonight, I'm going to take my dinner to the garage and eat it there! Remember our not-during-dinner rule, unless there's a crisis. You seem really upset, so let's talk in the living room when we've finished eating.

Crucially, Jim didn't declare the topic off-limits or minimize its importance. Rather, he asserted his need to have some space from the conversation and to shift when and where it would take place.

Rule #31

TELL YOUR PARTNER HOW YOU NEED HIM TO LISTEN

One of the things I love best about my husband, Steve, is that he is silly and funny, even about the most serious things that have happened to us. There is hardly a subject he can't make me laugh about. But the downside of his gift is that sometimes he jokes around when I need him to be serious and listen. I let him know this, though sometimes I have to tell him several times before he gets on board. ("I'm not in the mood to joke around. I need you to *really* listen to me now.")

It's not realistic to expect your partner's undivided attention and emotional presence for all conversations. When you really need a different quality of attention from him, let him know.

It may also help to tell the "listening partner" what you'd like from him, even before you start to talk: "I only want you to listen and tell me what I did right." "I want to hear your perspective and any advice you may have about what I should do next." "I only want you to try to empathize with how hard this is for me, even if it isn't hard for you."

> Give your partner a break and tell him directly what you want.

We might want our partner to magically know when we need his undivided attention and what sort of response we'd like from him. It's not fair, however, to expect him to mind read or pick up on nonverbal clues. Give your partner a break and tell him directly what you want from him in the listening department.

Don't hesitate to give him concrete feedback when he doesn't listen well enough. ("When I brought up the problem I'm having at work, you were looking around the room. Then you changed the subject and started talking about your bad knee.") Keep the criticism specific. It won't help to say things like "You never listen to me." In fact, that response may guarantee he never will.

You can also take the opportunity to ask your partner how well *you* listen, especially when it's a high-twitch subject. He may share something useful or surprising.

FOUR

CALL OFF THE CHASE:
HOW TO CONNECT WITH
A DISTANT PARTNER

I was thumbing through a magazine in an airport gift shop when I came upon an article on intimacy that included a questionnaire for rating your relationship on a 1–10 scale of distance and closeness. Before you fill out such a scale and then decide to hide under the covers because your relationship is a big failure, please know this: Some couples are happy being glued at the hip, others are happy living like cordial roommates, and others are happy wherever they may land between these extremes. There is no "correct" amount of closeness or distance that fits every couple, or even fits one couple for all time.

Of course, distance can be a red flag, signaling that trouble is being swept under the proverbial rug or that one person has checked out of the relationship. But distance doesn't always mean that the state of your union is shaky. Your partner's aloofness may simply be her way of trying to get through a

difficult time. Or, if you're raising young kids, perhaps neither of you can do much more than fall into bed exhausted
every night. Sometimes survival, not intimacy, is all we can
realistically aim for. In such times, the "solution" may be
realizing there's no problem at all—no matter what the marriage experts say. If life has plunked too much in your path,
you may deserve a medal of honor just for getting through
the day.

What's important is striking a balance between separateness and togetherness that works for both your partner and
yourself. That's easier said than done, because individuals
have different needs for closeness and distance. Moreover,
when we're upset by the other's unavailability, we may automatically go into "pursuit mode," which only makes the problem worse. If you chase a distancer, he will distance more. If
you distance from a pursuer, she will pursue more. Consider
it a law of physics.

Pursuing and distancing are normal ways that humans
navigate relationships under stress. A problem occurs only
when the pattern of pursuing and distancing gets entrenched
and the pursuer and distancer become polarized in painful
ways. When this happens, the behavior of each partner pro-
vokes and maintains the behavior of the other. For example,
stress hits (say, a problem with a child), and she moves toward
him, wanting to talk about it. He withdraws, which only raises
her anxiety, so she pursues more, which increases his distancing. Later a fight ensues, and each blames the other for causing it. It's always easier to point the finger at our partner than

to acknowledge our own part of the problem. In order to truly connect with a distant or distancing partner, you need to identify the cycle and take steps to change it.

Of course, each partner can both pursue and distance at different times or over different issues. For example, he may pursue for more emotional intimacy but withdraw around a medical issue. Regardless, the pursuer is the one in more distress about the distance, and therefore the one who is most motivated to change the pattern. The distancer may feel unhappy about how things are going in the marriage, but he's still more likely to maintain the status quo than move toward a partner who is in pursuit mode. For this reason, most of the rules that follow are directed at helping the pursuer call off the pursuit and find ways to reconnect that won't intensify the pursuer-distancer dance.

Rule #32
IDENTIFY YOUR ROLE IN THE DANCE

To change your part in the pursuer-distancer dance, you need to understand the characteristics of each style. Identifying our role is easiest to do at times of high stress, when we tend to become a more exaggerated version of ourselves.

PURSUERS . . .

- react to anxiety by seeking greater togetherness in their relationship.
- place a high value on talking things out and expressing feelings, and believe that others should do the same.
- feel rejected and take it personally when their partner wants more time and space alone or away from the relationship.
- tend to pursue harder when a partner seeks distance, and go into cold withdrawal when their efforts fail.
- may negatively label themselves as "too dependent" or "too demanding" or "too nagging" in their relationship.
- tend to criticize their partner as someone who can't handle feelings or tolerate closeness.
- approach their partner with a sense of urgency or emotional intensity when anxious.

DISTANCERS . . .

- seek emotional distance via physical space when stress is high.
- consider themselves to be self-reliant and private persons—more do-it-yourselfers than help seekers.
- have difficulty showing their needy, vulnerable, and dependent sides.
- receive labels such as "unavailable," "withholding," and "emotionally shut down" from their spouse.
- manage anxiety in their marriage by intensifying work-related projects or withdrawing into technology or sports.
- tend to give up easily on their partner ("It's not worth trying to discuss things") and have a low tolerance for conflict.
- open up most freely when they aren't being pushed, pursued, or criticized by their partner.

Keep in mind that it's the *pattern,* not the *person,* that's the problem in the relationship. Understanding the pattern and your part in it is the first step toward breaking out of it.

Rule #33

DON'T TRY TO MAKE A CAT INTO A DOG

You may have paired up with someone who is a private person—who doesn't want to debrief after every dinner party or talk in detail about the symptoms of his stomach flu. If so, don't count on the power of your love or your nagging to create something in him or her that wasn't there to begin with. When we interpret genuine difference as a problematic distance, we can end up making things worse.

One therapy client, Phyllis, was married to Doug, a quiet, introverted guy, who was an only child in his first family. She herself came from a "big, loud, glommed-together family," as she described it, and she was drawn to Doug's coolness, his quiet independence, and his singular passion for his work and his students. No doubt he was drawn to her extroverted nature and her large, colorful family.

Later in the marriage, as often happens, she resented the very qualities that drew her to him. She began to anxiously pursue her husband for closeness, now reframing his love for his work as "workaholism" and catastrophizing about his failure to share more of his inner life ("I don't know how we're going to make it if you never open up about your feelings"). Phyllis noted that Doug retreated further in response to her judgmental and critical pursuit, but now she felt that his coolness was an indictment of her.

I suggested that Phyllis think of her husband as a cat, and try not to take his need for separateness personally. Phyllis loved her cat, who, in keeping with typical feline behavior, would sit on her lap and purr contentedly, then jump off for no apparent reason and curl up in a corner. When her cat wanted space, Phyllis didn't anxiously ask herself what she had done wrong, or why he wanted to get away from her just then, or whether this signaled an impending disaster in their relationship. Nor did she try to force him back on her lap, knowing he'd only jump off again. She accepted his behavior as part of his essential catness, and she saw his moves toward and away from her as about *him*, not about her.

This shift in attitude didn't "solve" Phyllis's wish for more closeness in her marriage. Rather, it helped her remember the good qualities in her husband that had attracted her in the first place. As Phyllis took Doug's need for privacy and space less personally, she was able to calmly invite more connection rather than anxiously demand it. He, in turn, warmed up quite a bit, though he never turned into an overeager puppy.

Rule #34
DON'T JUDGE THE DISTANCER

Pursuing and distancing are patterned ways that humans move under stress, two different ways of trying to get comfortable. Obviously, relationships go best when neither partner is locked into the extremes and both have the flexibility to modify their style. But neither style is "right or wrong," "good or bad," "better or worse."

That said, it's natural to see our style as the correct one. If our way of handling a problem is to go into therapy, we may be convinced that our partner needs to do the same, even if he comes from a family with a strong tradition of figuring out problems on one's own. If we want to pay a professional to talk about it—well, he should too.

Consider a conversation between newly married friends of mine, Alan and Sabra. I was with them when Sabra received bad news about her sister's health, and no one was surprised when Sabra shared the information in a matter-of-fact way and then changed the subject. This was typical of Sabra, who had great difficulty sharing the softer, more vulnerable side of herself—a style that irritated Alan immensely, although he also admired her "Don't grumble, carry on" approach to life.

Later in the evening, Alan said, "As always, Sabra, you leave me no room to respond to the painful news you're sharing. It's like you have a broom in your hand and you're sweeping me away at the same time you're telling me about your sister's diagnosis. And then you're on to the next subject. You don't even give me the space to say how sorry I am that this is happening."

"Alan," she responded in her very firm way, "I *know* you're sorry that this is happening. I don't need to hear it."

When Alan began to argue the point, Sabra stopped him with an even firmer tone. "Look, Alan," she said. "When *you* talk about what's bothering you, you feel better. When *I* talk about it, I feel worse. I want to say it and move on. You need to appreciate this difference between us."

Alan needs to appreciate the difference *and* help Sabra understand that he needs space to respond when she shares painful news, even if she prefers that he stay mute. They'll do better if they can each modify their own style a bit while respecting their differences.

For my part, it was useful to hear Sabra say that talking left her feeling worse. Her words reminded me that even "clashing styles" obscure a basic human commonality. When stress hits, we all try to get comfortable. There is no one right way.

Rule #35

MAKE A DATE, NOT A DIAGNOSIS

When our partner has distanced, we have an understandable
tendency to diagnose him ("You've been absent lately; I
think you're depressed and don't
know it") along with the relationship ("I think the closeness
has gone out of our marriage").
If we're feeling vulnerable, we
also tend toward exaggeration ("We haven't had a real conversation in a year"). In this way, we can name a nonexistent
problem into existence or make a small problem into a large
one.

> Instead of talking
> about how you don't
> talk—just try talking.

When you want more connection, suggest an activity.
("I hear there is a beautiful trail by the lake—do you want to
check it out this week?") Instead of communicating about
communication—talking about how you don't talk—just
try talking.

Here's an example of what to avoid if your intention is to
get more connected with a distancer:

Carol described her husband, James, as unavailable for conversation, so she was pleased when he enthusiastically accepted
her suggestion to go out for dinner at their favorite Japanese
restaurant. They were chatting along fine, until the miso soup
arrived and Carol felt the need to "process" how their marriage
was going. By her own report, the conversation went like this:

*She: You know, I'm feeling sad that we don't talk any-
more.*

*He: What do you mean we don't talk? I was just telling you
what happened at work.*

*She: But I mean we don't really talk. Not really. Not the
way we used to.*

He: What do you mean really talk? I was just talking.

*She: Well, I never know what you're really feeling. I mean,
superficially, yes, maybe about your work. But at a
deeper level, I feel like you've shut down.*

*He: (angry) So you invite me on a date and now you're
criticizing me? That's not acceptable.*

*She: Please don't get defensive. Now you're acting like I'm
the problem because I want to be closer to you.*

*He: Well, what I want is to get out of here. This isn't my
idea of a date.*

*She: (angry) Well, this is great. I tell you I want to be closer
and you want to go home. That's really terrific.*

The evening was a disaster, which Carol blamed entirely
on James's defensiveness. He was, indeed, defensive, but
Carol had a more difficult time seeing her own contribution
to the downhill slide. If she wanted to "really talk," she might
have asked James more questions about his work, or initiated
a different conversation that they both might have enjoyed.
Instead Carol made negative comments about James ("I feel
like you've shut down") and about their marriage ("We don't

talk anymore"). This was, after all, a Saturday night date—
not a meeting they'd set up to discuss their communication
issues.

Before you try diagnosing your partner or your relationship, try initiating closeness, as Carol did when she set up the
dinner date. Refrain from framing your partner or your marriage in a generally negative light. The same advice goes for
the distancer. Instead of diagnosing your partner as overly
emotional or in-your-face, just try to close the distance.

Rule #36
LOWER YOUR INTENSITY

Getting out of pursuit mode may mean ratcheting down your level of intensity—which includes loud, fast-paced speech, interruption, overtalking, and offering help or advice that isn't asked for. This is not to suggest that these are neurotic traits or that you have some kind of personality disorder. A different partner, with a different cultural background, personal history, sibling constellation, and temperament might enjoy these very same qualities. He might view himself as lucky to have found such an articulate, impassioned, energetic partner.

Many distancers, however, are viscerally allergic to intensity and become more so with time. They may say "I don't like to talk," but they've actually stopped talking because they fear getting trapped in a conversation that feels awful to them.

If your complaint is "He won't talk" or "She won't talk," check yourself on the intensity meter. Remember that even positive intensity can also lead to more distance once the pursuit-distance dynamic is in place. Being intensely generous or solicitous (frequently asking if your partner is okay, showering him or her with praise, wanting a "real kiss" rather than a peck on the cheek while your partner is cooking dinner) is unhelpful when a distancer is feeling crowded. Lowering intensity doesn't mean shifting it from negative to positive—it means turning it off.

Experiment with a low-intensity style for a couple of weeks. Talk more slowly and less often, say it shorter, lower the volume, refrain from any interruption, avoid criticism, and leave more physical space. You can aim to do this in all conversations, or, alternatively, only around a particularly hot issue that you and your partner can't talk about for ninety seconds without getting polarized. See what you learn about yourself or your partner if you damp down all communication from, say, an eight to a two on a ten-point scale.

Rule #37
TRY OUT A "NEW YOU"

Sometimes you have to pretend less intensity in order to become less intense. It may feel phony to pretend to be calm when you're not, or to stop pursuing a distancing partner you believe needs to be confronted. But remember, you can't know what's true or possible in your relationship (or in yourself) until *after* you shift your habitual ways of moving in that relationship.

> Get creative about lowering the intensity between you and your partner even if it's the last thing you feel like doing.

Get creative about lowering the intensity between you and your partner even if it's the last thing you feel like doing in the moment. If you know you're going to be pressing your partner for conversation if you stay home, go out with a friend. If you're at the movies with your partner and feel angry that he's not taking your hand or even acknowledging your presence, talk only about the film when you leave the theater, not about your hurt feelings. If you're in the habit of hovering or "overseeing" things when he's preparing dinner, folding laundry, or putting the kids to bed, go to a different room where you can't observe what he's doing. Don't text or call unless you need to. You will eventually feel some of the calm you were only pretending to possess.

Rule #38
TURN OFF YOUR STUPID "SMART PHONES"

Modern technology, meant to keep us all connected, creates distance in couples even when we're not aware of it. Every couple needs to have technology-free time to experience each other with full, undistracted attention.

People become convinced that they have to take that call while they're on the beach, and that they'll advance more quickly at their job if they're available on e-mail at all times. Rarely is this entirely, or even mostly, true. Nor do you always need to be checking the news, the score, your e-mail, or anything else. And calling or texting a partner unnecessarily when he or she is out with friends is not just rude but also potentially hazardous to the relationship. We all need some mate-free space.

> It's good to have "time-out" rules from anything you're prohibited from using during takeoff and landing in an airplane.

Sit down with your partner and make rules for technology-free time. The rules in my marriage are

1.   iPhones off and out of sight during food preparation and eating meals, and no answering landlines.

2. no taking calls when we're in the middle of a conversation or we have people over—calls can be returned later.

3. if it's absolutely necessary to take a call, do so out of earshot of others.

It's especially important to unplug from technology if your partner complains about it. A client of mine made a significant improvement in his marriage when he informed his wife that his new rule was "No technology of any kind for two hours after leaving work and coming home to you and the kids." The change was especially meaningful because his wife, for good reason, was highly reactive to his BlackBerry. She once threw his BlackBerry in the toilet when she really needed his help getting dinner ready and he wouldn't stop texting his brother. This action comes with a "Don't try this at home" tag, although it did get his attention.

These days, it's good to have "time-out" rules from, say, anything you're prohibited from using during takeoff and landing in an airplane. Only *after* you've become disciplined enough to carve out technology-free time will you realize how the seductive lure of technology can separate you from your relationship—and from yourself.

Rule #39
PURSUE YOUR GOALS, NOT YOUR PARTNER

One of the most important challenges facing a pursuer is to shift the focus away from the distancer and toward his or her own life—and to do this with dignity and zest. Not only will this help the pursuer lower her intensity over time but it's also about the only way the distancer will recognize his own needs for more closeness or conversation.

Try this experiment: Set aside at least a few weeks to stop focusing on your partner. Put 100 percent of your energy into your own life. Stay warmly connected to your partner, but don't ask for more closeness; in fact, forget about closeness for the duration of this experiment. Resist any temptation to invite him to move toward you. Take your worries and conversational needs elsewhere. You might even give him a little more space than he's comfortable with by adding new activities or spending more time with your friends and family.

> Becoming self-focused is one of the most effective ways to break the pursuer-distancer dynamic.

Desist from criticism and negativity. Don't mention his lack of warmth, interest, and attentiveness. You might even offer an apology for earlier behaviors. ("I'm sorry I've been on your back recently. I think part of the problem is that I've been under stress and I've been avoiding figuring out what I need to do in my own life.")

Most importantly, stay warm and kind, which may require you to fake it at first. Resist the temptation to either fight or to swing into a cold, reactive distance. A frosty retreat will not change the pattern, although he may temporarily go after you. Refocusing your time and energy into your own life does not mean becoming emotionally unavailable.

During these weeks, focus on the quality and direction of your own life. What talents or hobbies might you want to develop? What are your work goals? What are your values and beliefs about being a good sister, brother, daughter, son, aunt, or uncle? What connections do you want to build in your community? Do you want to make new friends or spend more time with old ones? Are you exercising, eating well, and otherwise taking good care of yourself? What sort of home do you want to create? What brings you pleasure or joy? Are you being useful to others? This last one is perhaps the greatest of all antidotes to getting overly focused on what you're not getting from your partner.

Becoming self-focused is one of the most effective ways to break the pursuer-distancer dynamic. The best way to work on a relationship always includes working on yourself, so this experiment will put you on firmer footing no matter how your partner responds.

Rule #40
HEED THE DANGER SIGNALS

If you have followed all the previous rules in this section and your partner's distance still feels problematic, don't stick your head in the sand. It never helps to ignore a problem when you know something is seriously wrong in your marriage. At these times just focusing on yourself or trying to make fun plans does more harm than good. Instead, you need to open a conversation about your concerns, without anger and blame and without anxiously pursuing your partner for more togetherness than he wants.

When does distance signal danger? Your partner may be refusing to talk about an essential aspect of living together, like how money is being managed and spent, or how household- and child-related tasks are divided. Or perhaps his distance results from depression, or a dysfunctional behavior, such as an addiction. He may suddenly announce a desire for more distance than you can comfortably live with; for example, he wants to go alone to India to study yoga for a year. Or maybe distance has turned into stonewalling, meaning he's basically removed himself from the relationship and you just can't reach him.

You need to use both wisdom and intuition to know when you can't comfortably live with the status quo. When you feel you can't, it's vital to speak up about your concerns. Keep the conversation going over time, without getting back into pursuit mode. If nothing changes after a reasonable period, it's time to figure out your bottom line. The rules in chapter 8 will help you with this challenging task.

Rule #41
DISTANCERS, WAKE UP!

Most of the rules in this chapter have been addressed to pursuers, who have more pain and thus more motivation to make a courageous act of change. If you're the distancer in your marriage, you may feel pretty comfortable staying put. Or, more accurately, you may be unhappy in your relationship, but moving toward a partner in pursuit mode feels like jumping out of the frying pan into the fire.

Distancers rarely take the initiative to change the distance-pursuit pattern, but believe me, it's worth being the exception to this rule. Keep in mind that your distance is actually encouraging pursuit. The very qualities that make her "impossible to talk to" may have a great deal to do with the fact that she feels she can't reach you. She may feel that her voice and pain can't affect you, and that she's no longer your number one person.

Also keep in mind that distancing and stonewalling are good predictors of divorce. Many women, exhausted by years of pursuing and feeling unheard, leave the marriage suddenly. When a distancer fears that his partner may actually walk out, he may flip into a position of intense pursuit. But it may be too late.

Here are five fundamental ways to modify your role as "distancer."

1. *Take space, not distance.* If you need space, take it in a way that won't trigger pursuit. It's one thing

to work on a project in the garage when you've
made a plan to do so, and another to just disap-
pear into the garage as soon as your partner gets
home from work. Be as reachable for her as you
would be for a top business client or a very close
friend.

2. *Move toward her.* Review the rules for warming
   things up (chapter 1) and overcoming your listening deficit disorder (chapter 3). Give her
   your attention, appreciation, and full presence.
   Consult her about problems you face at work or
   in your family, and value her feedback. Tell her
   how you appreciate the contribution she's made
   to your life.

3. *Recommit to fairness.* If there is an unequal sharing of housework and childcare, take the lead to
   figure out how to make it fair. Notice when the
   house and the kids need attention. Notice when
   the kids' laundry is getting moldy in the washer.
   I cannot exaggerate how many marriages rise and
   fall on the unfair division of labor in family life,
   and how often this inequality triggers the pursuer-
   distancer dance.

4. *Confront her.* If she's "too difficult" to talk to,
   don't write her off, concluding that you've married the wrong person. If you're in the marriage

now, put both feet in it. Request the specific behavioral changes that will make it easier for you to talk to her. Tell her what you need—and tell her for as long as it takes. Most "pursuers" would rather be confronted by a strong partner with a clear request for a behavioral change than be met with silence. A firm, constructive complaint at least lets your partner know that you care about making the relationship better and that you're willing to fight for it.

5. *Say "Enough" to technological pursuit.* If you feel your partner is constantly pursuing you via technology, try leaving your phone at home while you take a walk or meet a friend for coffee. Tell your partner, of course, when you plan to be cell-free and when you're going to turn it off. Those of us who are old enough to have grown up before the age of cell phones realize how rarely you actually need to have one on your person.

Finally, keep in mind that extreme pursuit, like extreme distance, signals trouble. Yes, a strong warning is in order. You need to move toward the pursuer in a loving way *and* be clear about the limits of your tolerance. If you enable behavior that feels suffocating, or that leaves you chronically resentful, your marriage will go downhill, as will your own well-being. So speak up now. Give your marriage a fighting chance.

FIVE

FIGHT FAIR!

Have you ever gone home at the end of a difficult day and taken it out on your partner? Of course you have. It's perfectly normal to take in whatever stresses life brings, and then to take them out on your partner. After all, what's a partner for? He or she is right there on the scene and the one with whom you are least likely to "watch yourself." And of course, your mate will inevitably do something to provoke you, even if it's how he holds his spoon or how she flosses her teeth.

Marriage is the lightning rod that absorbs anxiety and stress from all other sources, past and present. When marriage has a firm foundation of solid friendship and mutual respect, it can tolerate a fair amount of raw emotion. A good fight can clear the air, and it's nice to know we can survive conflict and even learn from it. Many couples, however, get trapped in endless rounds of fighting and blaming that they don't know how to get out of. When fights go unchecked and unrepaired, they can eventually erode love and respect, which are the bedrock of any successful relationship.

Anger, of course, is an important emotion. Our anger can tell us that something is not right and that we need to make a change on our own behalf. But fighting doesn't change the problem from which our anger springs. Quite to the contrary: Ineffective fighting protects rather than protests the existing relationship dynamics. When tempers flare, our capacity for clear thinking, empathy, and creative problem solving go down the drain. We get overfocused on what our partner is doing to us (or not doing for us) and underfocused on our own creative options to move differently in our relationship. We use our "anger energy" to try to change our partner, and, as a result, nothing changes at all. It's remarkable how many couples can precisely describe their particular pattern of painful fighting, and equally remarkable how many feel helpless to change it.

The rules that follow are intended to help you be flexible and creative, which is not the same as being stuck in the role of the passive or "one-down" partner. They will give you the tools to stop the fights and negativity that can threaten your marriage or simply ruin an otherwise good day.

Rule #42
MAKE YOUR OWN RULES

The first rule about fighting in marriages is to make rules for how you as a couple will treat each other. Make rules that you are responsible for following even in the heat of the moment. We often act as if the intensity of our anger gives us license to say or do anything, because,

> Happy couples are not couples that don't fight.

after all, we're way too furious to be able to stop what's coming out of our mouth! Of course we *can* stop ourselves and behave better that is if we have a genuine intention to have a better marriage. If you or your partner can't keep your anger from getting out of control, it's important to get professional help.

There's no shortage of advice from experts about how to fight fair in marriage. I suggest you begin by sitting down with your partner and coming up with a few rules of your own. These might be, for example, "No yelling or name calling," "No bringing up past grievances during a fight," and "No bringing up problems at bedtime." Many couples find it helpful to keep a written copy of the rules in a place where both will see it daily.

Happy couples are not couples that don't fight. Rather they're couples that fight fair and take responsibility for their own words and actions, no matter how furious they may feel inside.

Rule #43

ADOPT A DISTINGUISHED BRITISH
HOUSEGUEST

Most couples have more control over fighting than they think they do.

Years back I saw a high-powered, professional couple in San Francisco who went at each other's throats, verbally speaking, 24-7. Everything turned into an epic battle—whether the issue was eating meals, having sex, planning vacations, spending and saving money, decorating the house, rearing kids, or dealing with in-laws and ex-spouses. When they fought, they "kitchen sinked it," revisiting one old hurt after another, and never resolving anything.

Thus far, nothing had helped them calm down. Both claimed they were powerless to control their tempers. Then a distinguished British professor came to stay with them as their houseguest for several months, living in a guest room adjacent to their bedroom. "During that time, we never raised our voices," the wife told me. "We were pretty courteous with each other. Pride, I guess." They both agreed it was the best several months of their marriage.

> Most couples have more control over fighting than they think they do.

I wish I had a distinguished British houseguest to loan out to my high-conflict clients. It might be a useful exercise to imagine that you have one of your own. Like the couple in San Francisco, you might learn that you, too, are capable of adjusting your behavior. It's all about motivation.

Rule #44
STOP IT!

You will have a better marriage if you make a sincere effort to keep fighting and negativity from escalating. Instead of waiting for your partner to do the right thing, you can take the initiative to add a note of humor or calm into a downward-spiraling conflict.

John Gottman uses the expression "repair attempt" to refer to any statement or action—silly or otherwise—that does the job. He gives the example of a couple fighting about whether to buy a Jeep or a minivan, with the conflict escalating into the higher decibels. Suddenly the wife sticks her tongue out in perfect imitation of their four-year-old son, and the husband, anticipating she's about to do this, sticks his tongue out first. The tension melts as they both start laughing.

> True victory lies in stopping the fight, and making your point at a calmer time.

This specific strategy might sound silly, but Gottman's research indicates that the failure to initiate a repair attempt—or the failure to *respond* to a partner's repair attempt and give her a graceful way out of an argument—is a flashing red light that signals danger to the survival of your relationship.

Of course, we want our partner to be the one to de-escalate first, especially if we're convinced that he "started it" and is the one to blame. We lose sight of the fact that true victory lies in stopping the fight, and then making your point at a calmer time. It doesn't matter whether you use humor, or touch, or a simple refusal to participate by saying something like "If you want me to listen, get out of your debate posture!" The repair efforts you make to change the tone (or volume) of an increasingly nasty exchange can, over time, save and strengthen your marriage.

Rule #45
ACCEPT THE OLIVE BRANCH

If your partner takes the initiative to de-escalate, do your best to accept the offer to stop the fight or repair the disconnection.

Early in our own marriage, Steve and I fought a lot, and we'd ultimately stomp off angry to separate parts of the house. Usually, I'd stew for about five minutes and then go find him.

> It takes only one person to end a fight. It takes two people to heal the disconnection.

"I'm really sorry," I'd say. "I apologize for my part in this." Most often, Steve didn't accept my apology. He'd tell me it wasn't genuine, that I hadn't truly given sufficient thought to my behavior, and that I just wanted to move on like nothing had happened, and so on.

This is a common way fights continue when they could de-escalate. One partner refuses to accept a gesture of reconciliation because it doesn't feel authentic or it lets the other person off the hook. Of course, when Steve refused my gesture, I'd stomp off myself.

Eventually, I figured out a better way to handle things. When Steve rebuffed my apology, I'd say, "Okay, I'm going to think more about my part. And I'll wait for *you* to come to me when *you're* ready to talk." Interestingly, it didn't take long before Steve would come find me and take the initiative to repair things himself. He'd say, "This is stupid, let's just try to let it go." Or, "Let's drop it now and we'll talk about it another time." In sum: Steve was lousy at accepting my initial repair attempt. After he rebuffed me, however, he was great at offering the olive branch, and I was good at accepting it. Repair accomplished!

It takes only one person to end a fight or refuse to participate in it. It takes two people to heal the disconnection that follows a fight and move forward. Ideally, you should work on both offering the olive branch and accepting it—in whatever form it's handed to you. But if one of you is great at offering and the other at accepting, that can work too.

Accepting a peace offering does not mean that you are finished talking about a painful issue. Nor does it mean that you must forgive your partner for deception, or betrayal, or plain old unfairness. "I'm sorry, please forgive me" isn't a sufficient repair when serious harm has been done in your marriage. Accepting the olive branch simply means that you agree to end a fight or negative interaction and try to move forward with goodwill. This way, you'll open a space for the possibility of later conversations on the very subject you may still be angry about.

Rule #46
"LEAVE ME ALONE!" MEANS "LEAVE ME ALONE!"

Ideally partners can call an end to escalating fights before
they get out of control. In real life, however, things can go
from zero to one hundred before one person realizes they
should have exited the conversation earlier. When an argument has degenerated into a screaming match, or one person
has absorbed more emotional intensity than he or she can
manage, stop the interaction immediately.

When your partner says "Leave me alone," do it. Force
yourself to get away. You can offer one invitation to keep the
conversation going. ("I'm sorry
I was being obnoxious. Can we
try again? I promise to lower
my voice.") But if your partner
still wants to be left alone, force
yourself to get away. This means
no following her to a different room, no slipping notes under
the door, no calling or texting, no adding one more word to
the conversation until you've both calmed down.

> When you've reached
> a certain level of
> intensity, no rules
> apply except this one.

When you've reached a certain level of intensity, no rules
apply except this one. Even pursuing your partner with the
intention of clarifying your position or apologizing is coun-
terproductive when he has reached his limit or she has reached
hers.

The partner who stops the fight should take the initiative

to revisit the subject within twenty-four hours, unless the issue was really small and stupid. Stop rules ("Leave me alone") don't work well unless each party knows they can reopen the conversation at a later time.

Rule #47

HONOR YOUR PARTNER'S VULNERABILITY

Many of our most persistent fights arise when one partner fails to honor the vulnerability of the other. It's important to learn about your partner's vulnerabilities and sensitivities, which usually have their origins in the family he grew up in, or other painful events that she—like everyone else—doesn't just "get over." Perhaps your partner can't stand being misunderstood, or being treated as ignorant, or being touched in a particular way. You can make your own list.

Don't try to talk your partner out of her vulnerabilities (impossible!) or prove to your partner that he or she is being oversensitive (makes things worse!). Instead, try to deepen and refine your knowledge of your partner over time. Learn more about the family that your partner grew up in by inviting her stories of the good, the bad, and the terrible, and by getting to know her family members when possible. This kind of intimate knowledge deepens your connection and can help you lead with your heart and not your attack dog.

Alicia, a financial planner whom I saw in therapy, told me that she and her partner, Mary, fought every single time they left a party or social gathering. "Mary claims I'm paying attention to everyone but her," Alicia told me. "I *live* with Mary! Of course I want to talk to people I don't get a chance to see. She's being totally illogical. This is obviously all about Mary's family history, where she was always the invisible outsider."

Alicia's interpretation of Mary's behavior may be accurate. There is nothing logical about how partners respond to each other in long-term relationships. Everyone brings their pain and unresolved longings from their first family into their marriage. We all overreact, based on our past, to certain of our partner's traits, qualities, and behaviors. If Mary was the invisible outsider in her first family, of course she wants Alicia to really *see* her and to pay attention.

With the help of therapy, Alicia was able to stop fixating on how unreasonable Mary's expectations were. It turned out to be easy enough for Alicia to talk to her friends at parties *and* pay attention to Mary. She made it a point to sit next to her on the couch awhile, to draw her into one or two of her other conversations, and to show physical affection in a manner that Mary appreciated.

I'm not suggesting that you give in to unreasonable demands when doing so is at your expense. Rather, I'm suggesting that you look at a partner's complaint from a wider perspective and tend generously to your partner's vulnerability. People enter marriage with a deep longing (usually unconscious) that their partners will tend to their wounds and not throw salt in them.

Rule #48

APOLOGIZE

Tendering a genuine apology when an apology is due can go a long way toward repairing a disconnection following a fight. It can also restore our sense of integrity and well-being when we believe we've done something wrong. It's important to know that we can make mistakes and behave badly and then repair the disconnection. Without this possibility the inherently flawed experience of being human would feel impossibly tragic.

A true apology needs to be sincere and not just a quick way to get out of a predicament or a fight. Nor does it help to apologize with a grand flourish and then continue the very behavior you are apologizing for, whether it's coming home late from work or not leaving your partner space to talk in the conversation. Passionate expressions of remorse are empty if you don't put sincere effort into ensuring that there is no repeat performance.

Don't apologize with a "but" ("I'm sorry, but you . . ."). "But" automatically cancels out an apology and nearly always introduces a criticism or excuse. And don't apologize in a way that shifts the focus from your actions to your partner's response ("I'm sorry that you felt hurt by what I said last night"). Own your behavior and apologize for it—period.

It takes courage in marriage to be accountable, to see ourselves clearly, and accept responsibility for our part of a negative interaction. Don't get caught up in "who started it" or who is more to blame for the fight. Sometimes anger and resentment melt away when one person can simply say "I'm so sorry for my part in this." A willingness to apologize is often contagious. It models maturity for your partner and improves your ability to work together as partners.

Rule #49

DON'T DEMAND AN APOLOGY

If you're married to someone who doesn't apologize, it won't help to doggedly demand it. Instead, try to understand that some people can't or won't offer a genuine, heartfelt apology even if you deserve one. They won't follow the previous rule even if you Xerox it and tape it to the bathroom mirror.

There are many reasons why certain very decent people can't apologize. For example, your partner may be a perfectionist, so hard on himself that he doesn't have the emotional room to apologize. Or he may have too much shame to say "I'm sorry." People need to have fairly decent self-esteem to view their own less-than-honorable behaviors clearly and apologize for them.

Or your partner's experience growing up in his first family may have made the act of apologizing too emotionally loaded. One man who wouldn't apologize to his wife or children told me this: "My parents were always in my face to get me to apologize to my brother and always assumed everything was my fault." His folks would say, "You apologize to Scott right now!" Then, "That wasn't a *real* apology. Now say it like you mean it!" He found the process so humiliating that his solution as an adult was to never say he was sorry. If his wife insisted he owed an apology, he'd withdraw into silence or grumble "I'm sorry" as a way to get her off his back.

Almost everybody has a hard time apologizing if they feel "overaccused," that is, pushed to assume more than their fair share of the blame. As one man put it, "When my wife criticizes me, I don't want to apologize because I feel like I'm putting my neck on the chopping block. If I apologize, I'm agreeing with her that I'm the whole problem. And that's not true." If your partner experiences offering an apology as a blanket statement of his culpability or inadequacy, he won't be able to do it.

Do request an apology if you think it's due. Talk with your non-apologizing partner over time to help him understand how important an apology is to you. Try to learn more from him about why apologies are not forthcoming. But don't get into a tug-of-war about it. An entrenched non-apologizer may use a nonverbal way to try to defuse tension, reconnect after a fight, or show you that he's in a new place and wants to move toward you.

Rule #50
BE FLEXIBLE: CHANGE FOR YOUR PARTNER

As I've said in *The Dance of Anger* and elsewhere, it's not possible to change another person who doesn't want to change. It's also true that folks in successful couples change for each other all the time. If two best friends accommodate each other to be fair and to make a living arrangement go more smoothly, why wouldn't we do the same for our mate?

My husband, Steve, is a pretty good model of flexibility. If I want him to change something, he usually changes it, whether it's his shirt or the music he just put on. If I have "a thing" about something—say, I like to arrive very early at the airport, and not a minute late if we're meeting someone at a restaurant—he makes it a point to accommodate. If I criticize him in a harsh tone when I'm having a hard time, he considers the hard time I'm having and lets my burst of obnoxiousness slide right by him.

Of equal importance is the fact that Steve doesn't accommodate on things that matter. He's by no means a wishy-washy guy. It's just that my happiness, and the tone of our relationship, matter more to him than a whole lot of little things that really don't mean much to him at all. Because of his generous track record of flexibility, I have an easier time being flexible myself when he stands his ground.

Women have historically been advised to please their man—and at great personal cost—rather than rock the marital boat. And many men accommodate too easily because they are conflict-avoidant. Don't confuse flexibility (born of strength and high self-regard) with submission (born of fear and low self-regard). Too many of us refuse to budge on minor issues because we think it's a sign of weakness to accommodate, as if our relationship were some kind of competition that we can't afford to lose. Ask any athlete (or blade of grass, if you can find one that talks): Flexibility often trumps sheer force.

Rule #51
DON'T THREATEN DIVORCE

Don't threaten to break up in the heat of anger, which is neither helpful nor fair. Nor should you bring up divorce as an attempt to scare or shake up your partner. And surely you don't need to mention splitting up simply because it passes through your head now and then. Many married folks entertain fantasies about divorce yet are far from acting on it. Few things hurt marriage more than communicating that you have one foot in the relationship and one foot out the door.

That said, it's very important to talk about divorce or separation if you find yourself *seriously* considering it, even ambivalently. It is devastating to a partner to be left, and it is far more devastating if it hits him "out of the blue." We owe it to our partner to communicate clearly when we are questioning whether we can stay in the relationship if certain things don't change. But remember that divorce and separation are serious subjects, which are best discussed at calm times and not words to be flung about in the heat of anger.

It's essential to have a very long-range view of marriage and feel confident that the relationship can weather the tough times that will surely be there. Both partners need to know that marriage can weather huge amounts of stress and conflict without the long-term commitment being constantly at risk. Indeed, if you threaten divorce or separation with any frequency, it will become an increasingly likely outcome.

Rule #52

YOU CAN LOSE IT!—BUT VERY, VERY SPARINGLY

There are times when showing your partner a raw expression of hurt and rage will break through his defenses and get through to him. Important addendum: This will happen only if your outburst comes as a big surprise to both of you, meaning it's a rare event and not the rule.

A therapy client of mine, Kathy, discovered that her husband was having an emotional affair with one of his grad uate students. Some instinct led her to go into the "Deleted" box of his e-mail, where she found his provocative and sexualized messages. He'd written, for example, "I didn't dare hug you when you left my office Monday, because I didn't trust that I'd be able to stop myself there." It seemed that they hadn't (yet) had sex.

My client confronted him immediately, and they had endless conversations about the situation. My client said all the right things and expressed the whole range of feelings that were evoked by reading the e-mails. She took a clear position on what she expected from her husband, and how much he was putting at risk if he didn't stop the flirtation. Probably she said all that could be said.

Kathy was a therapist herself, and she talked like one. She felt it was important to take a position calmly, to speak in "I" language, and to keep the intensity down so as to ensure that her message be heard. The problem was that Kathy almost always talked this way. She was, by nature, a very low-key person, who didn't have much range in her speaking style. Teasingly, her younger sister sometimes called her "one-note Kathy."

One evening in their bedroom, Kathy simply lost it. She began screaming at her husband about the graduate student. "It was the kind of screaming that left my vocal cords raw," Kathy told me. I was afraid I might have actually damaged them." After she screamed for maybe a minute or less, she threw herself down on the floor of their small bedroom closet, sobbing uncontrollably, refusing her husband's pleas to come out or at least open the closet door. She slept in another room that night.

This episode got through to Kathy's husband in a way that all the previous conversations had not. The rawness of Kathy's emotional response opened his heart in a way that his wife's calm "I" language and "good communication" had never done. "Losing it," to use Kathy's term, turned out to be both good and, perhaps more to the point, unavoidable.

> A raw show of emotion may get through to your partner at a deeper level.

I'm not suggesting you should make a plan to "lose it." I've lost it this way perhaps three times in four decades of marriage, and certainly not by plan. There is, however, an exception to every rule of good communication. When "losing it" is a very rare and surprising departure from your usual fighting style—and does not harm your partner—a raw show of emotion may get through to your partner at a deeper level.

Rule #53
BEWARE OF THE FOUR HORSEMEN!

When couples are stuck in fighting and negativity, I sometimes tell them about John Gottman's research on "the four
horsemen of the apocalypse." These are the attitudes and
behaviors that can erode and ultimately destroy a marriage.
Of course, these villainous horsemen show up in the best of
relationships. But when they take up permanent residence
in a marriage—and when the couple fails to repair the
damage—Gottman reports that he can predict divorce with
an accuracy rate above 90 percent.

Study this abbreviated summary of Gottman's four horsemen (below). Having a recipe for divorce can help you become aware of whether you'd like to get one—or do the
opposite and build a better relationship.

HORSEMAN 1: CRITICISM
A criticism is a personal attack on some aspect of your mate's
character or personality. It differs from a constructive complaint, which addresses a specific action on the part of a
spouse. A criticism might sound something like "How lazy
can you get?"

HORSEMAN 2: CONTEMPT
Contempt can be conveyed in many forms, including name
calling, sneering, eye rolling, mockery, hostile humor, sarcasm—
any nasty or mean-spirited attempt to put the other person

down. For example, she complains that he's late for dinner, and he snaps, "What are you going to do, sue me?"

HORSEMAN 3: DEFENSIVENESS

Defensiveness is a way of saying "The problem isn't me, it's actually *you*." In the face of a complaint, a defensive partner argues, counterattacks, brings up a mate's faults, and climbs further up onto high moral ground.

HORSEMAN 4: STONEWALLING

Stonewalling occurs when one partner tunes out the other and disengages from the relationship. A "stonewaller" turns away from his spouse, sits impassively like a stone wall, leaves the room, or communicates that he couldn't care less what his partner says or does. Gottman reports that people stonewall to protect against feeling emotionally flooded, and that men are more apt to stonewall than women.

An important postscript: Gottman reports that if a couple makes successful repair attempts and they meet the 5:1 ratio of positive to negative statements or interactions (see Rule #4), the four horsemen aren't lethal. Nonetheless, the best plan is preventive: When these hoodlums come knocking, don't let them in.

SIX

FORGET ABOUT NORMAL SEX

A cartoon shows two birds perched on a branch in a tree. One says to the other, "To tell the truth, I don't think I fly as much as I should."

Poor bird. Flying is a normal process. But this bird has the notion he's not up to snuff. Maybe he's bought the latest best-selling book called *"Birds Who Fly 24/7"* and his heart sank when he read how inadequate he was. Perhaps the message in the bird-improvement book was couched in terms of what "research shows," "brain science proves," "nature intends," or "God wants." How can an ordinary little bird question such awesome authority? Something must be wrong with him.

Clients I see in therapy are very much like that bird. They think something is wrong with them—or with their relationship—because they are not having sex as much as they think they should. If they're not worried about the frequency factor, they may worry about their performance, their "equipment," their lack of desire or desirability, or the fact that most nights they'd rather get a foot massage from their partner than "do it."

Of course, sex isn't anywhere as natural, normal, or easy for our species as flying is for birds. Countless forces from childhood onward can block authentic desire and load sexuality with anxiety, fear, shame, and confusion. The truth is that our erotic life is as unique as our fingerprints. It is something that every individual has to keep figuring out for herself or himself as he or she moves along the life cycle.

Humans are anxious and vulnerable about sharing their bodies, and it's an especially difficult challenge in marriage. For all the safety and security that coupling up can bring, it's not easy to have "good sex" (whatever that means) with the person you live with year in and year out. The countless books and products on the market that promise to restore passion to your sex life can leave you feeling worse than ever when they don't work. And the pursuer-distancer dance, when it takes place in the bedroom, can lead to an impasse so painful that both the pursuer (who tries to initiate sex) and the distancer (who isn't interested) dread getting into bed at night.

I hope the following rules will help you fire the sex-cops, especially those who have set up precincts in your head. These suggestions may also help you break a pattern in bed that's keeping you stuck. If reading any of these rules leaves you with a "down" feeling, ignore the rule. When it comes to rules about your own body and how you want to share it with your partner, you're the ultimate expert.

Rule #54
DON'T SAY "FOREPLAY"

The word *"foreplay"* is problematic, so delete it from your sexual vocabulary. The word suggests that whatever you do short of intercourse or orgasm isn't the "real thing" but merely something that you do to get ready for the real thing.

Who's to define the real thing? Sex expert Marty Klein says something like this: Suppose you and your partner go on a date to a fabulous restaurant that's known for its delicious desserts. You're both thoroughly enjoying the appetizer, the salad is pretty good, and the main course is terrific. When it comes to ordering the dessert, however, your server tells you that unfortunately they are all out. You turn to each other with bitter disappointment, fallen self-esteem, and a profound sense of failure. You thought you were enjoying the food and each other, but now you realize you had a sadly inadequate dining experience. You return home depressed. This, Klein says, is what it's like when people evaluate their sexual experience by what happens (or doesn't) at the end.

Sex surveys ask people how often they "do it" without taking into account the complexity of physical intimacy or erotic pleasure. Some people achieve orgasm pretty easily but have sex in a mechanical or impersonal manner. Other people may have orgasm infrequently, or dislike penetration, but love the intimacy, erotic pleasure, and physical closeness they share with their partner. They may enjoy kissing, cuddling, spooning, wrapping themselves around each other like pretzels and having a loving and playful, erotic connection in bed that's not focused on intercourse or orgasm. As one of my happily married friends put it, "If I had gotten hung up on having an orgasm, it would have become a big project and obsession, a distraction from the wonderful sex we always have."

Couples can have a strong erotic connection even when he can't maintain an erection, she doesn't want to try to have an orgasm, or when illness and disability take a toll on one or both partners. Aim for a flexible, light, ever-changing definition of what "having sex" means to you and your partner. Don't accept anyone else's definition of what constitutes real or good sex.

Rule #55
BE EXPERIMENTAL

Sex writer Susie Bright notes that adults exhibit childish reactions to sexual practices that are new to them, much like little kids who are offered a vegetable they haven't seen before:

> *"That's disgusting!"*
>
> *"But darling, you haven't even tried it."*
>
> *"I don't care. I hate it!"*

It's not a good idea to force yourself to do anything that repels you. At the same time, you may want to push yourself to be experimental, especially if you have a loving and generous partner.

Push yourself to be experimental, especially if you have a loving and generous partner.

Elizabeth, a therapy client, hated the idea of receiving oral sex. The idea was so distasteful to her that she ruled it out of bounds. This might not be a big deal—or could even be a relief to some men—but giving oral sex was incredibly important to her partner's erotic life and his sense of connection to her. Over and over he let her know that her refusal or inability to try was a terrible loss to him. He was also understandably upset that he always initiated these conversations.

Elizabeth never considered that it was her responsibility to open a conversation in which she acknowledged how difficult this loss was for him. After some years they both agreed not to talk about it, and Elizabeth's husband tried to mourn his loss.

One night Elizabeth had a vivid dream that her husband was having oral sex with another woman. In the dream he was telling this woman how much it meant to him. "Something turned in my brain when I woke up," Elizabeth told me. "I felt a profound sadness to think I had imposed this ironclad rule." Then she added, "And since it was *my* dream, maybe I was the woman in the dream—and maybe I should at least try to be that woman."

At first, Elizabeth had to push herself to have oral sex. It never became her favorite thing, but to her surprise it became quite pleasant and, with time, pleasurable. Her husband, for his part, was delighted and grateful. Because one thing always leads to another, gradually they both became more experimental and imaginative in bed.

Don't wait till you have a transformative dream to hold these seemingly opposite truths in your mind at once:

"Don't force yourself to do anything sexually you really don't want to do."

"Try (for yourself and for your partner) to do new things that you think you don't want to do."

No expert can tell you how to choose between these two truths on any particular day. But you will benefit from trying to hold both in your mind with a sense of curiosity and possibility.

Rule #56
STAMP YOUR SEX FANTASY "NORMAL"

Whatever your sex fantasy is with your partner, consider it normal. Married people tend to go with "whatever works" to get aroused or to push themselves over the top. No one reaches orgasm by fantasizing that they are holding hands with their partner during a romantic, moonlit walk on the beach. Your partner may be your best friend whom you love more than anybody, but it doesn't necessarily follow that he or she is the one you're thinking about when you're trying to rev up your arousal or have an orgasm.

Making love involves two people, but having an orgasm involves a single individual who takes full responsibility for getting there. Some people sink into erotic sensation without fantasy. Others openly share their sexual fantasies with each other while making love. Other people think about outside attractions, or latch on to fantasies that are as odd and quirky and far-ranging as the human imagination in order to bring themselves over the top.

What you fantasize about may bear no relation to what you want in real life. You may boot yourself into an orgasm thinking of your dentist tying you down and ravishing you in the chair, but you'd run for your life if that situation actually presented itself. Nor are your fantasies a measure of how much, or how well, you love your partner. They evolve from a place in the unconscious mind that has nothing to do with your adult capacity for love and intimacy. They are not a sign of disloyalty to your partner, nor an indication that you are some kind of weirdo. Fantasies are just fantasies.

Rule #57
DON'T JUDGE YOUR SEX DRIVE

Comparing ourselves to others and concluding that we come up short may be the most common way humans create their own unhappiness. With sex (as with the rest of life), do your best to sidestep comparisons or, more realistically, strip them of their emotional power. It's true that people differ widely in the ease and intensity of their sexual experience, just as they differ in their capacity to enjoy conversation, music, friendship, or gardening. But so what?

For women in particular, arousal and orgasm can take a lot of time and attention after the altered brain chemistry of the honeymoon stage wears off. As marriage expert Pat Love describes it (referring to lower-testosterone women), first you have to focus, focus, and focus some more, until you get exactly the right erotic fantasy in mind. Then, of course, a spot on the ceiling (is it a water stain?) or a thought about the laundry distracts you (should I have put the linen pants in the washer?), and you have to start working all over again until finally, finally, you have your orgasm.

"Lack of desire" is too quickly labeled a medical problem, disorder, syndrome, or dysfunction.

I don't mean to discourage you from getting help if you're seriously troubled by a damped-down libido. It can be very difficult to relax, for example, if you've been sexually abused, and it's worth the money to see a good therapist. And a number of medications that shut down libido can be replaced by other medications that don't. Also, your capacity for erotic attraction changes with time, so you may lose it when you're home with little kids and rediscover it when they're in school and you're out in the workplace again. But don't compare your current level of desire to what it first was with your partner. Helen Fisher, a biological anthropologist, reminds us that the hormonal cocktail for passion and romance is short-lived, lasting a few years at most.

Certain physical conditions that inhibit sexual response can be helped by a skilled urologist or gynecologist. But "lack of desire" is too quickly labeled a medical problem, disorder, syndrome, or dysfunction, with the goal of getting you fixed. Be wary of a narrow medical model; sexual desire is far too emotionally complicated to reduce it to hormones and to the function or dysfunction of your parts. My best advice is to realize that you're okay the way you are, or, as Elisabeth Kübler-Ross put it, "I'm not okay, you're not okay, and *that's* okay."

Rule #58
DON'T WAIT TILL YOU'RE "IN THE MOOD"

If you wait to have sex until one or both of you genuinely want to have sex, you'll wait too long. The desire for sex easily goes into hibernation after marriage, and especially for women after kids. The more time you let go by before trying to have sex, the harder it will be to start up again. Many people have to push themselves to get started, but once into lovemaking they enjoy it and feel more connected. This is especially true if they can take all the pressure off themselves and their partner, and assume a "let's relax and just see what happens" attitude.

Pushing yourself to have sex once in a while can keep your libido from going into deep freeze, especially after children come along. There is often at least one person in a couple who will not feel a "natural urge" to initiate sex but may be able to get into it when he or she really tries. If you're not aroused, there's still something to be said for doing something for your partner's pleasure and being open to simply enjoying the physical closeness.

Rule #59
RAISE YOUR LAUNDRY CONSCIOUSNESS

If you want to have sex with the mother of your children, try this erotic tip: Share household tasks. If you don't, there can be trouble in bed. Not only will your partner be too tired for sex but she may also resent the unfairness of the situation (even if she denies it to herself, because women, after all, are *supposed* to keep the home running smoothly).

Family therapist Marianne Ault-Riché once gave a talk in which she outlined her tireless efforts to raise her husband's laundry consciousness, which involved getting him to ". . . not only put the laundry in the dryer because I asked him to but to *think* about laundry, to *wonder* to himself, as I did, whether damp clothes might be sitting there in the washer waiting to mold; or whether there might be shirts that didn't get taken out of the dryer before it stopped and were sitting in there getting progressively more wrinkled."

Marianne told the joke about a man eager to arouse his wife. He asks her to share her most erotic fantasy. After a moment's thought, the wife says, "I'd like for once to make love in a room where the toys are all picked up and the laundry is folded." "Great!" her husband replies. "Let's go next door to the neighbor's house." You'd better hold on to your sense of humor as you struggle with the challenge of domestic inequalities, because the subject is painful and serious when it goes unresolved.

Will a truly loving, equal partnership ensure that she'll

want to have sex with you? No, it won't. Sex has a mind of its own. Good emotional intimacy in couples does not guarantee good sex. But bad emotional intimacy does contribute to bad sex. If you are an unfair or ungenerous partner, you may well ensure a poor time in bed, with a partner who is too tired and resentful to make an effort to please you.

Rule #60

WOMEN: TELL YOUR PARTNER WHAT YOU WANT
MEN: TRY NOT TO BE DEFENSIVE

Keep telling your partner what you want, even though the conversation can be difficult and painful. Be patient with his making the same "mistakes" over and over, just as you'd want your tango instructor or Italian teacher to be patient with you. Some people have a natural gift for dancing or languages or tuning into a partner's sexual rhythms and desires. Most don't.

Women today may believe they're entitled to lay claim to their authentic desires, but they often decide it's easier to just get it over with. ("Yes, I fake orgasm because he doesn't enjoy sex as much if I don't.") Or they feel their partner is not teachable. ("Everything he does feels wrong. He can't change.") Or he is so defensive that conversations go straight downhill. (He ends up feeling that I'm telling him he's a bad lover. It ends in a fight.")

If you have an extremely mature sexual partner, he won't take your instructions ("Higher, lower, more force, keep doing *that*") much more personally than if you were telling him how to scratch an itch on your back. That's the ideal, but it's highly unlikely that you have such a partner, because humans are so vulnerable about their sexual "performance" and do take things personally.

You may also need to show and not just tell. A therapy client repeatedly told her husband to touch her "in a more mindful way" and to kiss "like kissing is a mutual dance" rather than something one person does *to* another. At first, there was a struggle. Her husband felt hurt, while she felt irritated that he'd seem to "get it" and then "lose it" a week later. After repeated kissing demonstrations on her part, over several months, he finally understood. Both partners need to be patient and forgiving when it comes to asking for a change, because it is extremely difficult for people to undo old habits.

When it comes to *coming*, you may have your own inhibitions about telling your partner what you need, especially if it doesn't match some picture you have in your mind. If you're not having orgasms, and this experience is important to you, try to get creative and speak up. You're the best guide, so tell him what you want, even if it feels very hard to say it and you imagine that other women aren't making the same request. ("After you've come, I want to touch myself here, and I want you to hold this vibrator and use it *this* way.")

> Not *all* sex is, or should be, a mutually intimate moment.

Don't get caught up in whether your partner *likes* doing it or not. Not *all* sex is, or should be, a mutually intimate moment. There is something to be said for altruistic sex. Your partner may begin to warm up to a new practice when it becomes clear how much pleasure it gives you.

Rule #61

IDENTIFY THE PURSUER-DISTANCER DANCE IN BED

When it comes to sex, it's quite simple to identify the part you play in the pursuer-distancer dance. If you keep trying to initiate sex and almost always end up feeling rejected, you're the pursuer. If you're the party who isn't interested and feel you can't make the effort, you're the distancer. Men are often (though not always) the pursuers for sex, just like women are often (though not always) the pursuers for conversation.

In the bad old days, some marriage counselors prescribed the following strategic solution to the "He won't talk"/"She won't have sex" impasse: The wife was given tokens to dole out to her husband in exchange for, say, twenty minutes of conversation. After the husband collected a certain number of

> Nothing will change if you keep trying to jump through hoops to initiate sex.

tokens, he could exchange them for what a colleague calls "a good *schtupping*" (Yiddish for intercourse). She would get her conversational needs met, he would get his sexual needs met, and all would be well with their world. Thankfully, this "therapeutic solution" has long been discarded.

Lesbian and gay couples get stuck in the same dance. One partner keeps pursuing until it's too painful, at which point he or she retreats into cold withdrawal. The sexually reluctant partner is too exhausted, too angry about something, worried that the kids may come in, isn't a "night person" or "morning person," or doesn't feel enough trust. Escaping traditional gender roles doesn't mean escaping traditional problems.

When the pursuer-distancer dance becomes rigidly fixed, both parties dread getting into bed at night. The bed becomes a place of tension and pain. The pursuer feels devastated by the constant rejection. The distancer may be afraid to even put her arms around her partner and be physically affectionate because this may be interpreted as a "mixed message" that she wants sex, which will then trigger some kind of uncomfortable or angry interaction. Out of bed as well, things are apt to go less smoothly than they might, and irritability runs high.

If there are two "yes" partners, or two "no partners," there's obviously no problem. On the other hand, one "yes" partner and one "no" partner is a problem so common that you can think of it as normal, which doesn't mean it's good for your relationship. If either you or your partner is in pain about the pursuer-distancer dance, you need to understand that continuing these moves will only bring you more pain. Appreciating the need to do something different is an important first step.

Rule #62
PURSUERS, STOP PURSUING!
DISTANCERS, STOP DISTANCING!

There's only one way to break the cycle. The pursuer has to stop pursuing for sex. The distancer has to stop distancing. It's as simple—and difficult—as that.

IF YOU'RE THE PURSUER

You really need to "get it" that nothing will change if you keep trying to jump through hoops to initiate sex, only to get rejected and then go into periods of cold, angry withdrawal. You have to stop pursuing. More difficult still, you have to gather up all your anger and hurt and frustration and put it aside. Angry withdrawal is just the flip side of pursuit and won't lead to change.

How can you interrupt the cycle? Choose a time outside of bed, when things are good between you. Tell your partner you want to talk with her about sex. Tell her warmly that it's important to you that the bed not continue to be a place of struggle and hurt, and you want her to know that you're going to stop all attempts to initiate sex. You might say "I hope that you'll initiate sex at some point, because I can't imagine living forever without it. But I'm going to take all the pressure off you, because it hasn't helped either of us. And if you're in the mood for a hug, a kiss, or a back rub, let me know. I promise we can do those things without doing anything else. The pressure is off." Keep the talk light and brief.

Then you need to walk your talk. Be warm rather than angry when you get into bed at night. If she wants a hug or a back rub, give her one—and force yourself to stop at that. Be appreciative of all physical and sexual contact without focusing on whether she is getting aroused or enjoying it. Never push her to enjoy sex, or have an orgasm, which only invites her to fake it. Men often say "I want her to *want* me," as if a partner's experiencing desire in a different way constitutes a profound rejection. Try to detach from this idea. Getting overly absorbed or focused on a partner's pleasure usually isn't helpful.

If, over time, she makes no moves toward you, keep the conversation going, but not at nighttime and definitely not in the bedroom. Let her know that you have no intention of going back to initiating sex, but you're feeling alone and frustrated. Ask for her ideas about how to solve the problem and listen to her without getting defensive. Keep the conversations short, as distancers tend to dread long sex conversations. Revisit it about every month if your partner does nothing. Finally, make sure you are being a fair, generous partner in all other respects.

IF YOU'RE THE DISTANCER

Initiate sex once in a while even though you don't feel like it. Your partner can't live in a sexless marriage, especially if he is someone for whom sex is an enlivening, essential force and means of connection. *To decide you won't be a physical partner because you don't feel like it is like his deciding that there will be*

no more conversation in the marriage because he's not a talker.
On the sex front, there is probably something you can do
that wouldn't be too terribly difficult.

If you don't want to have sex because your spouse hasn't
healed a serious betrayal or disconnection, or because he's
not being a fair or respectful partner, you obviously need to
address this with him. I'd never suggest having sex with
someone who treats you in a demeaning or disrespectful way.
But sometimes a standoff occurs when he is making an honest effort to repair a wrong from the past and the distancer
takes the attitude "I'm not going to have sex with him until I
really know I can trust him again." If your partner is a good
person, and is making an honest effort to repair a past harm,
try to make your physical connection part of the process of
healing, reconnecting, and restoring trust, rather than making it something your partner has to "earn back" over some
indefinite amount of time.

I understand that this rule, more than any other rule in
this book, may leave both partners feeling "I just can't do
that." If you truly believe that your relationship is sustainable
as a platonic friendship over years or decades to come, you
can forget about this rule. But if you know in your heart that
some sort of sex life is necessary for your relationship to survive over time, grab this rule and go for it.

Rule #63
NEVER TAKE MONOGAMY ON FAITH

When people marry, they take an oath to forsake all others. The vow is public because it's so hard to maintain. Humans are not "naturally" monogamous: Well over a dozen species of mammals (including wolves and gibbons) are more monogamous than our own. We tend to want both the security of a long-term partner and the excitement of someone new.

It's a myth that you can swear your partner to monogamy or keep him faithful by being the best lover and most gorgeous person in the world. In the realm of sheer physical attraction, no long-term partner can ever compete with the idea of someone new. Let's just say that affairs wash the brain in chemicals that trigger an altered, obsessive "high" against which marriage has no chance, erotically speaking.

It's also a myth that the "real reason" behind an affair is a faulty spouse or bad marriage. A sexually or emotionally distant marriage will definitely make an affair more likely. It's also true that affairs happen in the best of marriages.

Affairs have many sources. Many people begin affairs on the heels of an important loss, or at the anniversary date of an earlier one (your wife has an affair when she approaches the age of her dad when he died suddenly of a heart attack). Opportunity and work context are other huge factors. If your straight husband works a nine-to-five job with an all-male work crew, he's in a low-opportunity job as far as temptation goes. On the other hand, if he's a college professor, you may be able to count on a certain number of students doing every-thing they can to make him feel brilliant and desirable and otherwise primed for an affair.

The problem with taking monogamy on faith—even when, or *especially* when, your partner says, "I'd never be attracted to anyone but you, honey"—is that you will put yourself to sleep. You won't be awake to a real threat to your marriage, or even to the simple fact that your partner is a sexual being and outside attractions can't be stamped out of existence. The paradox is that affairs are *more* likely to occur with couples that assume their marriage is affair-proof. The very assumption shuts down conversation, lowers your moti-vation to improve things, and invites dishonesty.

Rule #64
SET LIMITS

When you feel threatened by a partner's relationship outside the marriage, speak up. You can't stamp out his desire for others, nor can you stop him from being unfaithful. But that doesn't mean that you have to shut up, or blind yourself to a potential threat, or take no position at all about your partner seeing a person who may be a temptation.

In my own marriage, the unspoken rules for "outside relationships" have varied with our age and stage of life. When we were a couple in our twenties in Berkeley, I was quick to encourage Steve to hang out or go to the movies with female friends, both because I thought nothing possibly could happen (he was too high-integrity a guy) and because I believed that couples should never constrain the freedom of their loved one where outside friendships were concerned. Fast-forward a few decades, and we're quite different. Neither of us is a paranoid maniac, nor do we deny or try to prevent the reality of outside attractions. But at several points in our marriage we've said "no" to one or the other continuing an outside "friendship" because we sensed it was going to end up at the expense of our marriage, even if the other denied it.

Many couples have a "don't ask, don't tell" policy about outside attractions. Other couples choose an "open marriage," usually with a set of rules to go along with it. (No sleeping with the same person twice, not with anyone in our friendship group, etc.) No expert has the right to assume she knows what boundaries are best for a particular couple. But if your commitment is to fidelity (my bias, for sure), speak up when you feel a threat. Don't be afraid to set limits on a particular outside relationship when your gut tells you that your partner could be tempted.

Rule #65
KNOW WHEN TO CLOSE YOUR GATE

If you're committed to being faithful, picture a circular gate around your personal/sexual self. Decide how open or shut you need to keep it in order to be faithful and present in your marriage.

One couple I worked with, both in their early thirties, were totally committed to monogamy. He kept his gate open a bit because he enjoyed flirtations and erotic exchanges with women he was in contact with, and he had a high level of free-floating sexual energy that added to his sense of vitality and attractiveness. He didn't take these encounters seriously or let them intensify. He just enjoyed his sexual energy as a natural part of life.

> Knowing how open or closed to keep your gate is a good way to stay faithful.

His wife was the opposite. While her libido was much lower, she was vulnerable to emotional affairs. Even if nothing happened, she'd get someone under her skin and start feeling obsessed in a way that made her less present with her husband. While she was the one in the couple with strong religious and moral convictions, she claimed to be helpless when an infatuation took her over. Emotional affairs, even when they never become physical, can be as intense and damaging to a marriage as an attraction that ends up with two people in bed.

When this couple talked about outside romantic and sexual attractions, it became clear that the wife needed to keep her gate tightly closed. Her emotional affairs were as threatening to her marriage as any physical affair her husband might be tempted to have. Her husband, for his part, needed to close the gate as soon as a flirtation threatened to become something more.

Knowing how open or closed to keep your gate, and being really honest with yourself and your partner about it, is a good way to stay faithful. The hard part is distinguishing between outside attractions that are simply enjoyable and life-enhancing, and those that may come at the expense of your relationship.

Rule #66

DON'T MAKE YOUR PARTNER'S AFFAIR
A DEAL-BREAKER

Nothing is more devastating than discovering that your pur-
portedly faithful partner had—or is having—an affair. The
fact that your spouse has lied to you (whether in words or in
silence) adds unspeakable pain to the sexual betrayal. If the
affair was ongoing, it's normal for the harmed party to feel
enraged, depressed, crazy, disoriented, obsessed with details
of the affair, and convinced that nothing will ever be normal
again. But as catastrophic as an affair can be, don't automatically make it a deal-breaker. If you and your partner have a
significant history together, and especially if you have kids,
try to work it out.

Keep in mind that an affair is not a terrible aberration
that occurs only in unhappy marriages. Affairs happen in
excellent marriages as well. I've seen couples heal from affairs
once they are out in the open; this can even enhance a couple's
communication and closeness. For this positive outcome to
occur, both parties need to be committed to each other, to
truth telling, to avoiding future temptations, and to walking
the long, bumpy path of healing and restoring trust.

If you've been the unfaithful spouse, consider the excellent advice of psychologist Janis Abrahms Spring, the
author of *After the Affair.* Her counsel: Never, ever encourage
your partner to "get over it." Instead, be available to hear
your partner's pain and take it in. Don't wait in dread for her

to bring it up again. Instead, open conversations yourself that let your partner know that you're continuing to think about the affair and that you won't leave her alone to carry the pain. Be totally present to hear her anger and sorrow for as long as it takes, which may feel like forever. Dr. Spring explains that if you want your partner to let go of her pain, then *you* have to hold it.

If you're the harmed party, consider couples counseling before filing for divorce on the one hand, or pushing yourself to forgive on the other. Give your unfaithful partner the chance to make reparations and earn back your trust. Give yourself and your relationship the opportunity to heal and grow stronger. This is slow and arduous work, no question. But if both of you are committed to healing, it can be worth the effort.

SEVEN

KID SHOCK:
KEEP YOUR BEARINGS
AFTER CHILDREN ARRIVE

No one can prepare you for how much your marriage will change after the first child enters the picture. It's not that kids change your marriage. It's more accurate to say "You will no longer have what you now call your marriage. You will have an entirely different marriage in an entirely different life." Until you have them, you simply can't begin to imagine how kids transform everything.

Many parents report that the addition of children deepens their connection. This is especially so if both parties are active, loving parents, and generous, nurturing partners—and the universe tosses them a fair measure of resources and good luck. Yet, no matter how great a blessing it is to go from two to three, in fact few events stress a marriage more than the addition of a new family member. In that magical moment when a son becomes a father, a daughter becomes a mother, and parents become grandparents, every family relationship is called upon to make major readjustments.

Despite your firm resolve to nurture your own relationship and not let child-raising issues come between you even while welcoming a new person to the family, it's always much harder than you think. Each child—and especially the first—brings with it an extraordinary level of change. Change, no matter how positive, is accompanied by anxiety and emotional reactivity. When reactivity is high, new parents may find themselves feeling walled off from their partner or at odds with each other without either one intending to start a fight.

Each new phase of child rearing—infancy, the school years, teens, empty nest, grown kids returning home or not leaving in the first place—will challenge your couple relationship in new ways—as will a child who faces unanticipated mental or physical challenges. Plus, everything from your own extremely imperfect childhood will be revved up. Then there is the matter of sheer physical exhaustion, which has never helped anybody's relationship as far as I know.

I certainly don't want to present a bleak picture of children's impact on marriage. In fact, I advise you to ignore all those news reports concluding that couples without children lead happier lives. Large-group research findings say nothing about the balance of joy and suffering a particular child will bring to you, and how your own relationship will be affected. Furthermore, your personal "happiness quotient" is quite simply beside the point when it comes to an experience as profound as having and raising children.

The rules that follow will help you think creatively about your marriage when a child enters the picture. The rules for stepfamilies are different, so more on that in chapter 9. What's similar is that it's normal to go back and forth from feeling blessed to stressed and "totally flipped out" in that magical moment when two become three (or more) and you suddenly find yourself in unknown territory.

Rule #67

DON'T TRADE YOUR PARTNER IN FOR THE BABY

In addition to feeling overwhelmed and frustrated with your baby, you may also love your child with a fierce physicality and depth that can make the other partner feel like a total outsider. Often it's the father who feels pushed to the margins, especially if the mother is breastfeeding. He may respond by distancing further into work, rather than trying to get more involved in parenting. He's likely to feel further rejected by his wife's predictable loss of libido, which isn't helped by the added stresses of interrupted sleep, unruly hormones, and the endless demands of babies.

If you're the dad, you may not acknowledge the loss you're feeling, even to yourself. Men are still thoroughly discouraged from recognizing or voicing their vulnerability, and it feels unacceptable to many men to acknowledge negative feelings about the presence of a new baby as everyone is saying, "Congratulations, you're a dad!" Instead you may decide the baby will be more "hers" while you put your nose to the grindstone to provide for the family. Your wife, in turn, may also consider the baby more "hers."

When mother and child appear to be a self-sufficient unit, it can be hard for the "outsider" parent. Of course, the outsider may become the insider when the child is a bit older. But if you're the one who does more of the nurturing now, make sure your partner knows that he or she is as valued, needed, and loved as much—if not more—as before you became parents. And start having sex even if you don't feel like it, because sex is an important path back to intimacy with your partner.

Rule #68

"NATURAL" PARENT: BACK OFF!
CLUELESS PARENT: STEP UP!

Men often tell me that their wives are "natural" mothers, especially when the kids are little. I typically hear something like "My wife is so tuned in to our baby that I defer to whatever she thinks is right, or however she wants things done." Flashing red light!

Although some parents are true "naturals" (especially if they grew up with younger siblings), most parents become competent only through experience and lots of trial and error. And the more the one parent "owns" the label of the competent one, the more incompetent the other will become over time. Watch out for this sort of seesaw pattern, and interrupt it sooner rather than later.

Dads (or whoever is home less with the kids): Don't respond to normal feelings of exclusion or incompetence by distancing yourself from decision making and the hands-on work of parenting. The more you feel inept or distant, the more you need to orchestrate one-on-one time with your child.

Don't get discouraged by how long it takes to develop confidence that you can keep your child fed, diapered, soothed, and alive at the end of the day. Also, take your own opinions and "instincts" seriously and voice them. When one parent always defers to the other on something as important as rearing children, it's not good for the marriage.

Moms (or whoever is home more): Ensure that your partner

has a lot of time alone with the baby, without your supervision, criticism, expertise, or excellent advice, unless he asks for it. If he's fumbling like an idiot putting a snowsuit on your flailing toddler, move out of viewing range. People who are struggling to gain competence become more anxious and less competent when they're being watched or when they're offered help they haven't asked for.

Shed your role as on-site expert. The more you're convinced that your partner can't be left alone with the baby without a long list of detailed instructions, the more you may need to "dumb down" and develop more *in*competence yourself. Be sure to solicit his opinion on how to handle situations with your kid. If your reflexive response is that he'd have nothing valuable to offer—well, you've lost perspective and you need to ask anyway.

Keep in mind your child needs both parents to be competent and engaged. It won't be to your child's benefit if only one of you feels like a fit parent. Of course, parents feel unfit much of the time, since the job description outstrips all human capacity. Consider it a matter of "more or less" and try to support each other's competence.

Rule # 69
NURTURE YOUR RELATIONSHIP,
NOT JUST YOUR CHILD

The idea that you have to pay attention to your relationship when a kid comes along is the sort of conventional advice you might find when thumbing through a magazine in the pediatrician's office. It sounds as simple as 1, 2, 3, but the problem is that you'll give yourselves ten reasons to not do 1, 2, or 3. So here's 1, 2, and 3, along with the excuses you'll make not to do them.

1. *Get babysitters.* Leaving your kid with a sitter is a big step. First of all, finding a good sitter takes energy and initiative, both of which will be in short supply. Then there's the worry factor. While it's normal to doubt your own competence to be a parent, it's a nightmare to doubt the competence of hired help, since you're not there to see what's going on and your child may be too young to tell you.

   As author Anne Lamott puts it, "You'll want to sit outside the house in a rocking chair, with a gun laid across your lap, like Granny Clampett, to protect your baby. And you really won't be able to because life is out there prowling around like a wolf and it's going to drive you nuts."

Live with the anxiety and don't let it stop you from finding a good sitter—or better yet, two. Some couples line up someone who comes regularly on Saturday nights, or, alternatively, on a weekday so they can meet their partner for dinner after work. Keep in mind that the longer you resist finding a good, reliable babysitter and separating from your child, the more difficult it will become. Avoidance only makes fear grow.

2. *Go on a date.* Once you have a sitter, you actually need to go on a date. Expect to have enormous resistance to this idea. First of all, you're too tired to go out—you'd rather just go to sleep. Second, money is probably tight, so it seems more logical to rent a video and watch it at home when the kids are asleep. Third, you may not want to go out with your partner, just the two of you, like you did before the first child came along. What do you have to say to each other that isn't child-related? What *did* you talk about anyway, before the baby came?

Just do it. It is important to occasionally go to a restaurant, a real movie theater, a free cultural event, or some other activity you enjoyed before you became parents. It doesn't matter if you have a ho-hum time, or end up arguing about the expense of the meal, because that's normal and you need to overcome your resistance to scheduling dates. You might even see what happens if you decide in advance to *not* talk about your child or child-related topics, or anything on the family to-do list. Not to push you, but perhaps it's best not to wait until your kid is filling out college applications before you realize that you and your partner forgot to go on a date.

3. *Give your partner alone time, away from you and the kids.* Whatever age your kids are, it's very important you give each other time off from family life. Again, you won't want to, because family time is important and you don't have enough of that. Still, give it a try. You'll be closer as a couple if you support each other doing individual fun things apart from the family. Plus, your kids will be closer to both of you if they have the opportunity to have alone time with each of you.

You can probably add to this list of how to try to shore up your depleted energy reserves so that you have something left over for each other. Getting kids to bed an hour earlier makes a big difference. Resisting withdrawal into your favorite technology helps, as does resisting the cultural pressure to have your child participate in more than one extra school activity. Finding someone who can clean your house—even once a month—also makes a surprising difference, as can springing for a hotel room without kids every once in a while. The hard part (beyond economics) is actually *doing* something. Don't be like the man who lies shivering in bed but is too tired to get up and go find himself a blanket.

Rule #70
KEEP NEGOTIATING "WHO DOES WHAT?"

The "Who Does What?" issue will rush to the surface after a baby arrives, even if it was never a source of tension before. The time-honored roles of "man the breadwinner" and "woman the nurturer" run so deep that it takes persistence to buck them.

Not that you *should* buck them if they are working well for you at a particular stage in the family life cycle. No one else can tell you what arrangement is best for you. Just keep in mind that nothing erodes intimacy faster than one or both partners harboring a sense of injustice around an unequal division of labor. Of course, you'll have the same "Who Does What?" challenge with a same-sex partner. The difference is that you figure it out without conforming to outdated gender roles, where she automatically rolls up her sleeves to do the hands-on work of child raising and home running, while he automatically sees parenthood as a signal to amp up his role as provider.

> Negotiation is not the same as complaining. It means that you state clearly, without fighting or blaming, how the status quo needs to change.

At every stage of the family life cycle, you may need to reassess your priorities, values, and life plan. If you're the one who is unhappy with the division of labor at home, take full responsibility for negotiating and renegotiating.

Negotiation is not the same as complaining. It's not about bringing up the unfairness of the past. Negotiation means that you state clearly, without fighting or blaming, how the status quo needs to change. If your partner is fair-minded and flexible, you might make a list of the specific chores that need to be done daily (cooking, cleaning the kitchen), weekly or biweekly (taking garbage out, washing and putting away kids' laundry), and periodically (arranging for household repairs). Together you can initial who is currently doing what, allowing both of you to clearly see the imbalance and figure out a new division of labor. If your partner is not fair-minded and flexible on this matter, it's better to start small and request one specific behavioral change.

In either case, resist the impulse to pull up the slack when your partner doesn't do his or her share. This means, for example, that if he forgets he's in charge of shopping and cooking dinner on Sunday and Thursday, you don't throw up your hands and grimly do it for him. You can have healthy foods around and let everyone make sandwiches when they get hungry. If it's his week to dust and vacuum, don't expect him to clean like you do—but do expect him to clean. Your partner will test out whether "you really mean it" when you say you need a new, more equitable arrangement. So don't let him off the hook. If you do, the old pattern will reassert itself in record time.

Some people genuinely don't mind taking the lion's share of responsibility inside and outside the home. When there's no problem, there is nothing to fix. But if you're feeing angry, it's best to not continue business as usual. The accumulated tensions and resentments produced by inequality and the failure to negotiate can make intimacy almost impossible.

Rule #71
SOLVE THE "COST OF CHILDCARE" DILEMMA!

It's not fair to assume the man will shoulder the burden of earning because that's what men do, or because he makes more money. As one man put it, "My wife considers herself to be a liberated woman, and she insists that I share equally in the household chores. But she thinks it's my job to support her, and that if she wants to stay home with the kids, that's her right, just because I earn more than she could. What kind of feminism is that?"

Point well taken. But later, this same man unwittingly discouraged his wife from taking a part-time job she was considering by subtracting the cost of babysitting from *her* potential salary and concluding she'd be making "almost nothing" going back to work. And, of course, he preferred her to be home with their toddler, a perfectly natural wish. His wife did the same subtraction and also concluded that the financial contribution she could make was negligible. It wasn't her dream job she was turning down anyway.

> Change the math. It may prove to be one of the best investments you both can make.

But with work, as with all of life, one needs to look at the big picture. A person often needs to work her way up before making a significant salary. And for both partners, participating in the adult world of work has many personal benefits beyond dollars earned. The satisfactions of work, as well as the woman's need to ensure her economic viability in an uncertain world, didn't make it into this couple's calculations.

Change the math. Subtract the cost of childcare from *his* paycheck (or from hers, if she's the sole breadwinner). That is, instead of counting every dollar for childcare against every dollar she might earn, have the conversation about family economics in a way that makes clear that childcare costs are a shared responsibility, and that opportunities (and challenges) of a paycheck job are equally shared. Even if the net effect on family income is the same, subtracting the costs of childcare from his paycheck shifts the conversation from demeaning her contribution to honoring it. Another way to do the math is to subtract the cost of childcare proportionally from each income. If he makes $80,000 and she makes $20,000, subtract 80 percent of childcare costs from his salary and 20 percent from hers.

Obviously many couples today don't have the luxury of "choice" in the work-family dilemma, and a couple is lucky to have one partner with a well-paying job. Often both partners work one or more poorly paying jobs just to keep the family afloat. But if you're in a situation like the one I've described, consider reframing the dilemma. The adjustment in the emotional math may prove to be one of the best investments you both can make.

Rule #72
DON'T LET THE INMATES RUN THE ASYLUM

If your kids run the show, you can bet that you and your partner will be chronically stressed-out. The two of you need to be in charge. That means you have to decide on rules and consequences, and enforce them.

"What could be simpler than that?" I asked myself before the humbling experience of actually having a child of my own. I was convinced that when Steve and I had children, we would keep them "under control," unlike the idiot parents we saw at the supermarket who seemed to be in a brain fog while their child shrieked and flailed in the checkout line. Becoming parents quickly cured us both of this arrogant attitude.

Folks who tell you that "taking charge" is a straightforward and readily attainable goal either don't have kids or have "easy children" who keep their rooms tidy and set the table without being asked. Kids come into the world with their own unique strands of DNA, and some have a natural predisposition toward compliance and responsibility. Parents of such a child may take full credit for her good behavior and fully believe that you and your partner can easily get your frisky, attentionally challenged, rebellious, and colorful children "under control" if you'd just set rules and consequences. As of yet, there is no known cure for this delusional condition except to swap children with them for a week, and maybe throw in a couple of teenage stepchildren for good measure.

As you aim to set rules and consequences, be patient

with yourself. It's normal to have trouble, not because you're an inept team but because you are human. Don't hide in the broom closet and keep your feelings to yourself, convinced that more mature parents, guided by their generous instincts, would know exactly what to do.

Agreeing on rules and consequences does *not* require you and your partner to see eye to eye—whether the subject is your child's bedtime, granting his wish to watch a vampire movie, or insisting that he finish his broccoli before getting two scoops of ice cream. There is no "right way" to rear kids. *What matters is that you respect each other's opinions and reach a consensus about rules and consequences that you both can live with, even if you don't agree.*

> Agreeing on rules and consequences does *not* require you and your partner to see eye to eye.

Then you need to be consistent in clarifying the rules and enforcing consequences while being open to revising your strategy along the way.

One reason it's so hard to work as a commonsense team is that couples get polarized under stress. He stands for "law and order," and she stands for "love and understanding." He buys only organic food and won't allow sugar in the house, and she criticizes his "rigidity" in front of the kids and slips them secret treats. He thinks saying "no" to children is the reasonable, mature thing to do, and she thinks he's stingy and controlling. He says black and she says white.

When partners get polarized around parenting, it saps

their energy and connection as a couple. The fact is, kids won't suffer from eating some sweets, or going without them, or from being raised by *this* parenting philosophy or by *that* one. They will, however, become anxious or act out if they become the relentless focus of intensity between two parents who can't reach some kind of creative compromise around rules and consequences.

Rule #73
DON'T GO IT ALONE

A hidden cause of stress in marriage and family life is an attachment to an outdated model of raising kids and being a family. Maybe you have a picture of everyone sitting down to dinner at six thirty P.M. and having the kind of civilized, uninterrupted conversations that you grew up with—or wish you'd had.

If that's what happens in your home, more power to you. If you find, however, a painful discrepancy between how you think it should be and how it is, you should know that you're not alone. Times have changed—radically—and "family time" has changed with it.

Dr. Ron Taffel, one of our nation's top child-rearing experts, describes "family mealtime" in the twenty-first century this way:

> *Even when family members are seated at the same table, everyone may be consuming something different— take-out Chinese, microwaved frozen pizza, salad with low-cal dressing—often in separate worlds. Fourteen-year-old Jenny is texting under the table while apparently answering Mom's question about a homework assignment. Ten-year-old Bart casually asks for someone to pass him "the fucking salt." Sixteen-year-old Adelaide warns her siblings and her mom to "stay out of*

my way because I'm PMS-ing real bad." . . . Jenny and
Mom begin a heated exchange about a midweek concert
with Jenny promising to be back "no later" than 2:00 or
3:00 a.m.

I e-mailed this description to my friend Jeffrey Ann, a
sixty-one-year-old mother of fourteen-year-old Alex. Jeffrey
Ann lives in one of my old hometowns, Topeka, Kansas, and
I thought Taffel's description probably wouldn't resonate,
since Jeffrey Ann is on the old-fashioned parenting side, in
my opinion. To my surprise, she told me that it helped her
with some rigid expectations that had frustrated her as a parent. After she'd gotten mad at Alex for refusing to eat what
the rest of the family was eating, he'd told her that his friends
said they got to eat whatever they wanted (Jeffrey Ann has
the rare family who eats dinner together most nights at six
thirty P.M.). In a survey in one of his classes, Alex found he
was the only one who ate regular dinners with parents. Without a reminder that we're in a new era, you may microman-
age your kids in the hope of getting them to conform to
some unrealistic picture of family life.

I'm not suggesting that you and your partner adopt a
"teens will be teens" point of view and allow cursing at
your table. Nor should you give up your efforts to make dinner a family occasion—without cell phones and other
technology—if that's important to you. It's just to remind
you that parenting is more complex in today's world, and

that, in turn, makes marriage harder. Especially if you feel caught on the shoals of family expectations from earlier eras, make use of the many excellent resources, such as Ron Taffel's work, on what it's like to raise kids in today's brave new world. Don't think you can do this all by yourself. You really can't.

Rule #74

DON'T MAKE YOUR PARTNER THE "BAD GUY"

Here's a scenario you might overhear on any city street: Little Susie pleads with her dad for an ice cream cone, and he says, "I'm sorry, honey, but I can't get it for you because your mom doesn't want you to have it." His tone implies that he'd really like her to have the ice cream, but he has to obey his wife. Subtly, he's siding with his daughter at the expense of his wife and their marriage. Or (less subtly), "Okay, but don't tell Mom, because she'll be mad at me."

It's fine for Little Susie to understand that her mom has stronger views about sugar than her dad does. And it's a collaborative move for Dad to agree to support Mom's rule for the simple reason that she feels strongly about it. But once he's agreed to the rule, Dad needs to say no to the ice cream without making his wife into the bad guy.

If Dad can't get behind the rule, he needs to reopen the conversation where it belongs—with his wife. He might say "I'm finding there are times when I'm just not comfortable enforcing the 'no sugar before dinner' rule. If I'm out with Susie and I want to get her an ice cream cone, I need the flexibility to make that call—even as we hold to the general rule." It's our responsibility to collaborate with our partner on rules we can support, not to side with our child as if we were powerless before our partner, the family dictator. And even if our partner feels more strongly about a rule than we do, once we agree to follow it, it's important to own the decision instead of trying to score points with children by encouraging them—explicitly or implicitly—to blame their disappointment on our spouse.

Watch out for this stealthy triangle in which you move toward your child at your partner's expense. The subject might be your five-year-old wanting ice cream or your thirty-five-year-old wanting to move back home ("Your mom says you can't move in with us, even though I want you to"). When you don't agree with your partner, revisit the conversation and let your thoughts be known. ("I understand your concern about Jon moving back here without a plan, but I'm not comfortable closing our home to him. Can we work out a list of things Jon would have to agree to before moving back in that would make you more comfortable with the decision?") Don't be overly accommodating and then invite your child to see you as the beleaguered partner of a difficult spouse.

> Watch out for this stealthy triangle in which you move toward your child at your partner's expense.

As tempting as it may be to let your partner be the heavy when it comes to providing limits and discipline, it exacts a cost on both your marriage and your relationship with your child. It makes your partner feel alone with hard decisions, and it breeds resentment. And even if you gain short-term points with your kids, you're actually sending them the message that you're not capable of acting like an adult. You can end up either losing their respect or becoming a role model that's not in their best interest to follow.

Rule # 75

BE KIND TO YOUR KIN—ESPECIALLY THE GRANDPARENTS

When a child enters the picture, every family relationship is called upon to change. Kids raise the stakes for how you treat your kin, especially parents and in-laws. Your behavior is your children's blueprint for family and will influence how you get treated when they grow up. How you navigate these adult relationships is the most important legacy that you leave your children. They are watching you.

Kids want nothing more than for all the important adults in their life to get along. If, for example, the tension is high between you and your mother-in-law, little Hannah is caught in a triangle. She will not be able to figure out her own relationship with her grandmother free from the tension between the adults. Kids need their grandparents, even if they see them infrequently and no matter what you might think of these people. And kids are especially attuned to how their parents treat their own parents.

Nor can you fool your kids just by biting your tongue and pretending to be civil. If you're silently seething because your mother-in-law has brought eleven-year-old Jason an electronic game after you've told her "nothing electronic," Jason will pick up on the tension. Even little children have radar for disturbances in the emotional field, and some are more sensitive than others. You may have one child who can let emotional intensity between adults float by her, and another who absorbs it like a sponge.

Always aim to lower your own intensity with the grandparents. Being calm and kind to grandparents is not the same as having an "anything goes" policy. To the contrary, you each need to deal directly with your own parents when they habitually do something at the expense of someone in your household or violate your ground rules. That is, you tell your mother to respect the "no electronic games" rule even if it's your wife who has the strong feelings about it. Of course you and your partner can speak up to your in-laws—but you won't get far if your partner disappears from the fray and lets you be the emotional reactor for the two of you.

Watch out for this common triangle: Two women (wife and mother-in-law) have the "problem relationship," while the man stays out of the action (see Rule #105). Triangles obscure the real conflicts, which makes it impossible to identify and resolve them. For example, the mother-in-law is actually angry about her son's distance, although she targets his wife. The wife is actually angry that her husband doesn't speak up to his own mother, but this marital issue stays underground because she targets her mother-in-law.

Wherever you find a wife and mother-in-law slugging it out, you'll find a son who's not speaking up to either his mother or his wife. If you change your part in this triangle, it will have positive ripple effects through your marriage and every family relationship.

Rule #76
DON'T OBSESS ABOUT GETTING IT RIGHT

Ease up on yourself and your partner when parenting isn't going well. At times of high stress, no one is immune from getting stuck in a "dysfunctional family pattern." Why should you and your partner be an exception?

When I was writing my book *The Mother Dance,* I undertook an informal research project with high school girls from several schools. What mistakes did their mothers make? I can collapse more than a hundred observations and poignant stories into a seven-point synopsis. These girls told me

- their mothers are too busy for them, or, alternatively, too focused on them.
- their mothers are too intense, or, alternatively, too distant.
- their mothers are too strict and rigid, or, alternatively, too much like a friend or peer.
- their mothers don't tell them enough, or, alternatively, they tell them too much. ("My mother tells me things about my dad I don't want to hear, then I feel guilty I don't want to listen to her problems.")
- their mothers lie to them, or, alternatively, they tell them more "truth" than one would ever want to hear.

- their mothers don't expect enough, or, alternatively, their love is too conditional. ("My mother
  told me she wouldn't love me as much if I were
  a lesbian, which made me feel that she didn't
  love me at all, because if she really loved me, she
  would love me even if I was different.")
- their mothers didn't really empathize, or, alternatively, the daughter itches and the mother
  scratches. ("My mom feels my feelings, and I
  hate that. When I'm down, she's down; when my
  boyfriend broke up with me last month, I was so
  upset, but then my mother got upset, and then I
  was doubly upset because I was upset about my
  mother being upset.")

The observations of these teenage girls remind us how
hard it is for any parent to "get it right." It's an insight that
might allow us to be more forgiving of ourselves and our partner when it comes to the overwhelming task of parenting.

Rule #77
REMEMBER THESE TEN SURVIVAL TIPS

1. *Don't go it alone.* We are here to help each other, and once you have children, you and your marriage will need all the help you can get.

2. *Avoid perfectionism like the plague.* You may deserve a medal of honor for just getting through most days. Perfectionism is the archenemy of parents everywhere. Mothers are especially vulnerable to feeling guilty for not meeting someone's impossible standard.

3. *Your children's behavior is not your report card.* While you do affect your kid's behavior, countless other forces influence it as well. As psychologist Ron Taffel points out, children are wired differently, and feeling guilty and responsible for their problems makes about as much sense as feeling guilty that your daughter is the only kid in her class who can't see the blackboard without glasses.

4. *Don't predict your child's future.* Your child's life will take many surprising and unexpected turns. Disbelieve any expert who makes doom-and-gloom predictions about your child. No one can know your child's future for sure.

5. *Expect children to rev up your most unspeakable feelings.* As the novelist Fay Weldon noted, "The greatest advantage of not having children must be that you can go on believing that you are a nice person; once you have children, you realize how wars start." It is quite normal to hate your children and your partner at times. Just don't act on it.

6. *Don't overfocus on a child.* If you focus too much on a child in a worried or blaming way, you're probably underfocused on other problems that need your attention—your marriage, your family relationships, or your own personal growth. Broaden your focus of concern.

7. *Live your own life (not someone else's) as well as possible.* How you conduct your adult relationships is one of the most important legacies you will leave for your children.

8. *Stay connected to your first families.* If you work on your relationships with your family of origin, it will help your marriage and your children. If you work on having a calm, cordial, and respectful relationship with your partner's family of origin, it will also help your marriage and children.

9. *Lower your anxiety and reactivity.* Do whatever it takes to achieve even a little more mindfulness

and inner peace. When our mind is wrapped around worry and fear, we lose the gift of the present moment, and we become poor problem solvers, as well.

10. *Expect to freak out.* At certain times, following the previous rule is about as likely as your becoming an astronaut. Anxiety will flood your body. Your hyperactive brain will wake you at three in the morning with terrifying pictures of your child's future. Know that this is normal. Don't wake up your partner to worry along with you, although you have a perfect right to resent him for sleeping so soundly.

EIGHT

KNOW YOUR BOTTOM LINE

Give-and-take is essential for a good relationship. As the Rolling Stones song goes, "You can't always get what you want." Things go a lot more smoothly when partners are flexible about accommodating each other.

Equally important, however, is the wisdom to know when not to give in and go along. Accommodating your partner isn't a good idea if doing so violates your deeply held values, priorities, and beliefs. Marriage suffers when we become so tolerant of our partner's behavior that we expect too little or settle for unfair arrangements. Sometimes we need to challenge the status quo by saying "Enough!"—and really meaning it.

What does it mean to really mean it? A true bottom-line position is not an empty ultimatum. It's not a threat that we throw out in anger ("Damn it! If you do that one more time, I'm leaving!"). It's not a desperate, last-ditch attempt to force a partner to shape up. It's not a mixed message, where our words say one thing ("I can't continue to take this") and our behavior says another (we continue to take it once things calm down).

Rather, a bottom-line position evolves from a focus on the self, from a deeply felt awareness of what one is entitled to, how much one can do and give, and the limits of one's tolerance. One clarifies a bottom line not to change or control one's partner (although the wish, of course, is there) but rather to preserve the dignity, integrity, and well-being of the self. A bottom line is about the "I": "This is what I think." "This is what I feel." "These are the things I can and can't do."

A bottom-line position is something you just can't fake or pretend or borrow from your assertive best friend. Everyone has a different bottom line, even though we may not know what it is until we're put to the test. There is no "correct" bottom line that fits us all. While there's no shortage of advice out there, neither your best friend nor your therapist can know the "right" amount of giving, doing, or putting-up-with in your relationship, and what new position you are ready to take on your own behalf.

The rules in this chapter cover a range of "bottom lines," from those that come up in the dailiness of coupledom ("You have to clean the kitchen"), to voicing the ultimate ("If these things don't change, I don't think I can stay in this relationship"). Consider each rule carefully, as you work to define a strong "I" within the "we" of your marriage. This challenge is at the very heart of having both a relationship and a self.

Rule #78
START SMALL

If you have been the overly accommodating partner in your relationship, it can be a major move to make even a small change.

Stanley avoided conflict at all cost in his marriage. He didn't say anything to his wife that would bring differences out in the open and disrupt their pseudo-harmonious "we." He couldn't recall the last time he said to her, "No, I don't agree with that," and then held firmly to his position.

Gradually, Stanley put his toe in the water and experimented with having more of a voice. For example, he told his wife that he would wear the shirt and jeans he felt like putting on, rather than always deferring to her taste or rules about proper dress ("You may be right that I'm underdressed for the party, but tonight I'm going for comfort"). He began

> Real change in marriage often occurs at glacial speed. But it's the direction, not the speed of travel, that matters.

to order from restaurant menus without her supervision ("I know this place is famous for fish, but I'm in the mood for pasta"). If asserting himself on these matters had felt too difficult for Stanley, he could have started with something even smaller.

Armed with new confidence from finding his voice on

small issues, Stanley took on a big one. For several years, he had taken calls from his mother only at the office because his wife couldn't stand her mother-in-law and wanted Stanley to have nothing to do with her. He kept his contact with his mother "semi-secret" to avoid his wife's anger. "It's not worth the fight," he'd tell himself.

It was a huge move forward when Stanley talked to his mother from home and dealt directly with his wife's anger and criticism. He told his wife that he knew his mother could be a piece of work, but she was still his mother and he needed to have a relationship with her. When the countermoves started rolling in ("You're going to have to choose between her or me!"), Stanley held to his position with dignity ("I love you both, and I need to have a relationship with each of you"). When his wife spoke contemptuously, calling Stanley's mother a "toxic bitch" and worse, he told her to cut it out. He said, "Look, I'm totally open to hearing what you think about my mother, but the name calling and insults have to stop."

You don't need to jump off the high dive in order to practice having a strong voice in your marriage. Move slowly and think small. This will allow you to observe the impact of each new behavior on your relationship, and to see how you sit with the anxieties that change evokes. Can you stay on track and deal with your partner's countermoves without getting angry and defensive and without returning to the old pattern?

Change is a scary business, even when we're actively seeking it. Some people are very ambitious about change and try to do too much too fast. They may then feel overwhelmed, which provides them with a great excuse for doing nothing at all. Real change in marriage—the differences that make a difference—often occurs at glacial speed. But it's the direction, not the speed of travel, that matters.

Rule #79
SHOW HER YOU MEAN IT

Sometimes taking a position in words won't exceed your partner's threshold of deafness. You may need to *show* you really mean it, whatever the "it" happens to be.

Here's a recent example from my marriage. Dirty dishes were piling up in the kitchen sink. It was my week to clean the kitchen, and Steve told me several times that the growing mess wasn't okay with him. When I continued to ignore him, he finally told me that until I cleaned up there would be no business as usual. So although I was eager to go to the movies that Friday night, Steve wasn't coming with me. Nor could I expect him to respond to my requests for help as he usually did.

I knew Steve really meant it because I know Steve. He didn't need to argue or lecture. Instead of going to the movies, he played his guitar and I cleaned up, motivated by a sense of fairness, and also by self-interest, because I needed Steve's help with my computer and I really did want to go out with him.

I don't mean to imply that Steve and I typically resolve our differences by taking bottom-line positions with each other about what we can and can't live with. It's not our style to let things go on for so long, or to go on strike if we don't like what the other is doing. Lightness, humor, and ongoing conversation usually get us through most small differences and more difficult impasses.

That said, we both know there is a line we can't cross, that there are certain behaviors that the other won't tolerate over time. Even when it's not spelled out, couples usually know each other's bottom line, just like kids know what they can and can't get away with. And like a kid, a partner may keep testing the limits until the other person says "Enough!" and really means it. That place is our bottom line.

Rule #80
DO LESS

Clarifying a bottom-line position requires us to get in touch with the limits of how much we can comfortably do or give. When our partner is unresponsive to requests that he or she do more, we need to find a way to conserve our time and energy. To say "This is all I can do" is an important position to define in a marriage.

Consider Lisa, who came to therapy complaining about her husband, Richard, who wouldn't help out at home despite the fact that both worked full-time. How did Lisa stop the old fights and clarify a new position?

First she chose a calm time when she felt good about him. She said, "Richard, you know I'm having a problem with the amount of work I'm doing in the house. Part of the problem is that I end up feeling resentful, because, the way I see it, I'm carrying more than my fair share of the load. An even bigger problem is I'm exhausted much of the time, and I need to find a way to have more time for myself." Lisa asked Richard for his thoughts and also told him specifically what she'd like him to do to help out. Richard said he'd do better. Several months passed, and he made no changes at all.

The day came when Lisa made her actions congruent with her words. She made a list of tasks she'd continue to do (for example, a clean living room and kitchen mattered to her, so she wouldn't let things pile up there) and a list of things she would no longer do and hoped Richard would take over. Then she shared the plan with Richard, who tested her for two months by sulking, complaining, and becoming an even bigger slob than usual. Lisa calmly held to her position without anger or defensiveness. She continued to do more housework, because a clean house was more important to her than it was to Richard, but she let go of the things she said she wouldn't do.

Lisa stuck to cooking only three nights a week and let Richard fend for himself the other nights and when he came home late. Lisa also found additional ways to conserve her time and energy. If Richard invited friends or colleagues to dinner, she didn't shop or cook for the event, although she was glad to help out. It was hard for Lisa to let Richard sulk, but I reassured her that as far as I knew, no one had died of sulking. Richard eventually started doing more, but even if he hadn't, Lisa had learned to do less.

Lisa took this new position in her marriage out of a sense of responsibility for herself, and not as a move against Richard. She shared her vulnerability and limits ("I'm too exhausted and depleted to keep going this way"), which wasn't easy for her. As a firstborn, card-carrying overfunctioner, it was not in Lisa's natural repertoire to share her needs in a soft way so that others could see that she needed help. Sharing her limits with Richard was an important step toward taking care of herself.

Follow Lisa's example. Keep in mind that change is a

process and doesn't occur in a hit-and-run conversation during which you announce what you will no longer do. As always, stay self-focused and use "I" language. If you're focused on shaping your partner up or getting back at him, you're unlikely to be an agent of positive change.

Rule #81
LIGHTEN UP AS YOU TOUGHEN UP

Taking a bottom-line position doesn't mean that you cross your arms in front of your chest and make heavy "I" statements in somber tones. Developing a nonnegotiable position comes from inner conviction, self-respect, and a healthy sense of entitlement and courage. To be heard, you may need to lower the volume and intensity rather than raise it.

If you're struggling to exceed your partner's threshold of deafness, the first order of business may be to nurture your relationship. Move toward your partner in a loving and generous way, following the rules in the first several chapters before rushing in to take a bottom-line position. Remember that your partner won't listen well when the overriding tone of the relationship is hostile, critical, or distant. Do your part to create a surrounding climate of love and respect.

Give voice to the positive, even when you're the critic. You might make a list of what you're grateful for about your partner, to help you lead off with praise before you tell him what you need to be different. Keep in mind that the best communicators can take very difficult positions with a light and loving touch.

Rule #82
PREPARE TO BE TESTED

If you take a bottom-line position that challenges the status quo of your relationship, don't expect to be greeted by approval and applause. Real change comes with resistance— so prepare for it!

"Countermoves"—our partners' attempts, conscious or unconscious, to push back against change—are par for the course when we change our steps in the familiar dance. To review family systems theory 101, the process of change goes like this:

> Real change comes with resistance—so prepare for it!

One person begins to define a clearer, more independent self, draws the line, or does something that challenges the roles and rules of the system. Anxiety rises like steam. Then the "countermoves" begin: You may be accused of behaving in a way that is disloyal, selfish, misguided, crazy, or just plain wrong. Your partner may become angry or depressed. Now your own resistance to change may kick in. You may abandon your new position, concluding that your partner is too difficult, fragile, angry, or depressed to handle the change you are attempting to make and the new position you have taken. The upshot: No change occurs at all.

Your job is not to prevent countermoves from happening, which is impossible, but rather to anticipate them and hold to your position without becoming defensive or attacking. Expect that things might get worse before they get better. Far from being a reason to abandon your position, this period of being tested is part of the process of change.

Rosie told her husband, John, that she could no longer keep his serious depression a secret from his family and their closest friends, as he had insisted she do for almost a year. "I'd prefer that you tell them yourself," she said, "but if you can't, I will." And she did. She felt, and rightly so, that treating a serious depression as a shameful secret was preventing John (and herself) from getting much-needed help. Plus the secret keeping required lying, both in words and in silence, and it was taking a toll on her.

When Rosie spoke of John's depression to his parents and a few of her own close friends, John was furious. He sulked, moped around the house, and threatened never to tell her anything again because she had violated his trust. At first Rosie panicked, believing that she had contributed to deepening John's depression. Anxious and confused, she retreated herself.

I encouraged Rosie to give John space to react, and not confuse his countermoves with the long-term effects of initiating the change. I also reminded Rosie of her reasons for taking a new position in the first place: The status quo was untenable for her. Nor did she think that the secrecy was really helpful to John. To her credit, Rosie listened well to John's anger without becoming defensive or apologetic. Instead, she lovingly and honestly reiterated the reasons for her position:

John, I understand that you're angry with me. In your shoes I'd probably be angry too. But I've been feeling increasingly scared watching you become more depressed, and none of my suggestions for what you might do have been helpful. My anxiety is so high that I can't continue keeping such a big secret from people who care about us both. And if, God forbid, you should hurt yourself or take your own life, I'd never forgive myself for staying silent. For my own sake, I need more people on the team. My hope is that we can all support each other and support you as well.

In time, John did seek help for his depression, although he went to his first therapy appointment with Rosie's footprint on the seat of his pants. He ultimately came to understand Rosie's bottom-line position ("I can't continue keeping such a big secret") as evidence of love and concern, not betrayal. But even if John stayed angry, Rosie took the high ground. She took a position based on her own best thinking, not on her fear of John's reaction. Rosie refused—for both her sake and John's—to be held hostage by his depression.

Rule #83
THINK BEFORE YOU LEAP!

Don't jump in to take a position that's not right for you. Your best friend may say "Just tell him no" or "Don't let him treat you that way," but remember, you are the best expert on yourself.

Brenda, a therapy client of mine, was furious at her husband, Glen, who wouldn't move his boxes of books and other belongings out of the garage, where he'd stashed them many months earlier, leaving no room for their car. A close friend leaned on Brenda to take a position. "Tell him if he doesn't clean the garage by the end of the month, you're taking his stuff to Goodwill."

Brenda followed her friend's advice and issued the ultimatum to her husband. Glen didn't move the boxes, and on the first of the next month, they vanished. Glen was furious, and Brenda ended up feeling guilty beyond all imagining. Her remorse gave her a handy excuse to settle back into her old position, which was to sacrifice too much of her self in their relationship. After all, she'd followed her friend's advice and it had made things worse.

Was the Goodwill solution "wrong"? Not necessarily. It might have been a fine position for her best friend, but it wasn't right for Brenda. If Brenda had taken the time to check in with herself, she might have found a solution that fit her own personality and values, not her friend's. Perhaps she would have hired a college student to help her put the boxes in her husband's study or in a storage space.

Alternatively, Brenda might have decided that she wasn't ready to do anything about the boxes. When we take a clear position on one issue, it inevitably brings up others. Perhaps Brenda didn't yet feel equipped to address the central issue in her marriage, which was not about boxes. Rather, it was about the fact that her husband typically ignored her legitimate requests and complaints, which made her feel alone in the relationship and without a collaborative partner.

If we're looking at someone else's marriage, the "right" position to take may seem obvious. But from the inside, where we live, establishing a bottom line can feel overwhelmingly confusing. You may start out feeling clear, only to find that a fog descends upon your brain when you don't get the response you want from your mate. Sometimes just acknowledging your confusion and deciding you're not ready to confront a problem in your marriage is an act of clarity and self-definition.

Rule #84
STAND LIKE AN OAK, BEND LIKE GRASS

A bottom-line position need not be written in stone. You can always reevaluate it as new information comes to light. "Really meaning it" doesn't mean you can't change your mind.

When Annette and Elena came to see me for couples therapy, Annette had one foot out the door of their three-year relationship. She said she could no longer tolerate the fact that Elena had not come out to her parents—that Elena was still pretending that Annette was her best friend and roommate, rather than her life partner.

> "Really meaning it" doesn't mean you can't change your mind.

"I can't live with Elena treating our relationship like a shameful secret," she told me in our first session. Annette's initial position with Elena was "If you don't tell them by Thanksgiving, I'm out of here!" After calming down a bit, she modified her position: "I'm not going to your parents' house until *after* you've told them." And then, only half jokingly, "Maybe I'll go to Thanksgiving and make the announcement myself at dinner."

When I did a genogram (a family tree) for each woman, a striking difference in family patterns emerged. In Annette's family, blood was thicker than water. In the end, family togetherness prevailed. No matter that Uncle Charlie had joined some weird religious sect. He was still family and was always invited to family events.

In Elena's family, in contrast, differences weren't tolerated. If you fought with a family member, that person might never forgive you or speak to you again. Elena's mother, for example, hadn't spoken to her older sister since their mother's death eight years earlier. She had never forgiven her sister for making unilateral decisions about their mother's care.

Elena's father, for his part, had cut off from his entire sibling group when he'd felt cheated out of his rightful place in the family business. He was also cut off from his grown son from a previous marriage. This pattern of cutoff stretched back at least three generations on both sides of Elena's family.

In therapy Annette gradually developed more empathy for Elena's dilemma. She understood that Elena feared she could lose her family by coming out. This didn't mean that Annette dropped her position entirely. She held her ground that Elena needed to be on a *path* of coming out. But now she appreciated the importance of Elena's being thoughtful and strategic about the process of coming out. It would require time.

For Annette, modifying her initial position ("Tell them now or else . . .") was not a sign of weakness or over-accommodation. To the contrary, it reflected her ability to be compassionate and flexible when presented with a broader perspective and new facts.

A bottom-line position can be firm without being rigid. Even if we start out with a nonnegotiable position, learning more may challenge us to reevaluate what we think and feel.

Rule #85
WHEN TO—AND WHEN NOT TO—TALK ABOUT DIVORCE

Nothing will erode your relationship faster than bringing up separation and divorce as part of your fighting repertoire. Marriage goes through many ups and downs, and during your "down" cycles, avoid conveying pessimism about staying together for the duration. Repeated negative pronouncements tend to be self-fulfilling prophecies. If you're married now, keep both feet in the relationship and give it all you've got.

That said, if you find yourself thinking seriously about separation or divorce over time (not just during fights), you do need to talk about it. Everyone has the right to know just how high the stakes are if they choose to continue to behave as usual. You owe your partner honesty so he or she will have the best chance of deciding whether the relationship means enough to make necessary changes (find a job, become a partner in housework and parenting, go into inpatient treatment for an addiction, treat you with respect).

I've seen many devastated men in therapy who tell me their partner left them "out of the blue." The women, however, feel they've been voicing their anger and dissatisfaction for a long time. Often both are correct. He hasn't listened well enough, and she hasn't expressed herself clearly enough. She might have made repeated complaints and then returned to "business as usual" rather than taking the conversation to whatever level was necessary to ensure she could not be ignored.

It's not fair to bring up the topic of divorce after you've already decided to leave and any changes your partner makes would be too little, too late. Marriage has much more potential for change than you may think, so keep these two things in mind: Get separation and divorce talk out of the conversation when you're angry, or when you're not close to acting on it. If you are seriously contemplating leaving, tell your partner before you've made an irrevocable decision. The following rule shows how to introduce divorce into the conversation, when you must.

Rule #86
WHEN YOU VOICE THE ULTIMATE, MAKE YOURSELF HEARD

To say "If these things don't change, I'm not sure I can stay in this relationship" is to voice the ultimate bottom line. If you really can't live with something, you need to make yourself heard, rather than conclude that the other person can't hear.

Sometimes your partner can't imagine that you'd ever leave because there's been a long history of complaints and threats that never truly challenged the relationship. If the survival of the relationship is truly at stake, you need to push the conversation to an entirely different level. The first challenge is to be clear within yourself where you stand, which isn't easy. Then you need to be clear with your partner, which may include writing him a brief note in your own handwriting (no e-mailing or texting for important subjects, please).

Consider Ruth, who came to see me because, as she put it, "I'm married to a sex addict." She discovered that her husband, Bill, had four affairs during their ten-year marriage, and she suspected many more emotional and physical affairs from checking his e-mail and tracking his whereabouts. Both agreed that his sex addiction left him powerless to have relationships with women that didn't lead to a physical or emotional affair. Bill was in individual and group counseling with a male therapist who specialized in this problem.

At the start of therapy, Ruth talked more about Bill's sex

addiction than she did about her own issues. She kept up with the literature and frequently gave Bill reading material, as well as advice. "I love him," she told me. "Sometimes I'm mad and sometimes I'm sad, but I know that sex addicts are often powerless to control their behavior."

In therapy, Ruth gradually stopped being the expert on Bill and instead focused on herself. She had a difficult decision to make: If nothing changed, how much longer could she live this way? A year? Five years? Ten? Forever? Ruth considered whether she could tolerate Bill's behavior even though it caused her pain. If this was her decision, she needed to emotionally detach and learn to live with it. This would mean retiring her ineffective efforts to change, criticize, educate, monitor, or mother Bill as she moved forward with her own life. If, alternatively, she was reaching the limits of her tolerance, her challenge was to make sure that Bill understood this. The latter was where she landed.

When Ruth recognized that she couldn't continue to be in a nonmonogamous marriage, it no longer mattered whether Bill's behavior was driven by his hormones, his brain chemistry, a traumatic past, or the phases of the moon. It made no difference whether Ruth called it sex addiction or sauerkraut. What mattered now was that she was in too much pain to stay in the marriage. Armed with this personal clarity, she defined her bottom line in "I" language over several conversations and without criticism or blame. She also bought a blank card and wrote this note:

> *Dear Bill,*
>
> *I'm writing this note because I'm not sure you're hearing me. I've mentioned divorce so many times that it may sound like just one more threat, but this is no longer true. You need to decide whether you can be monogamous and faithful. I know I can't continue for too much longer if you're not. On a 1-10 scale of readiness for divorce, I'm a 9. If nothing changes, and I discover another emotional or physical affair, I plan to call a lawyer to file for divorce.*
>
> *Love, Ruth*

Bill did more of the same and Ruth carried out her plan. She couldn't save her marriage, but she could, and did, save her dignity. She knew she had given Bill every chance of hearing her. While going through a divorce was immensely painful, it was, over time, much less painful than staying in a marriage that was eroding her self-respect.

Most of the issues we face in marriage aren't "deal-breakers," but the challenge of taking a bottom-line position is the same. You need to get clear with yourself about where you stand. If you're not exceeding his threshold of deafness with multiple conversations, change the medium to a handwritten card—and don't exceed two paragraphs. When you're aiming to be heard, go for brevity.

Rule #87
YOU CAN LIVE WITHOUT YOUR PARTNER

To define a bottom-line position, even on small issues, you must know you can live without your partner if need be. The strongest relationships are between two people who can live without each other but don't want to.

I'm not suggesting that holding your ground on key issues will likely lead to separation and divorce. To the contrary, relationships are most likely to fail when we *don't* address problems or hold our partner accountable for unfair or irresponsible behavior. And the ability to clarify our values, beliefs, and life goals— and then to keep our behavior congruent with them—is at the heart of a solid marriage.

> The strongest relationships are between two people who can live without each other but don't want to.

That said, it's difficult to navigate clearly within a relationship that feels necessary to our survival. Consider the workplace, for example. If you're dissatisfied with unfair circumstances at work, you can complain to your boss and request a change. You can state your beliefs about unrealistic or unfair demands, and what you would like to see change. But you cannot take a bottom-line position ("I'm simply not able to take on the extra work you gave me") unless you know that you can survive economically and emotionally without that job. Marriage is no different.

It's scary to really mean it. If we take a clear position on a seemingly small issue, we are likely to feel an internal pressure to speak to other issues in the relationship. As we become clearer about what is acceptable and tolerable to us, our partner will also become clearer about where he or she stands and what he or she will and will not do. When we move from nonproductive complaining to assertive claiming, we will begin to see both the self and the other in a sharper light.

If your partner communicates over time (through actions if not words) that he'd sooner get a divorce than seek treatment for his addiction, look for a job, or do the dishes, you may have some painful choices to make. Do you choose to leave? Do you stay and try to do something different yourself? If so, what? These are not easy questions to answer, or even think about.

While it's not helpful to leap to divorce talk, it *is* helpful to know in your own heart that you *can* make it on your own, if necessary. If you think you can't, put your energy into strengthening your own self and your network of family and friends—a good move whether you stay together or not. No marriage can thrive when it's based on fear. The best marriages are committed, but entirely voluntary, partnerships.

Rule #88

**IF YOUR PARTNER IS LEAVING YOU,
FOLLOW THIS PLAN**

Perhaps you're the one in shock because your partner has voiced the ultimate, or even announced it's a done deal. It's devastating when a partner expresses a wish for divorce or announces a plan to move out for a while to think things through.

If you're the party who is facing this terrible loss, you may feel an urgent need to pursue. You may want to text constantly or leave phone messages begging your partner to return. You may keep requesting more conversations to help you understand your partner's decision. You may promise to make any changes she or he has previously asked for. A strong emotional current may drive you to keep expressing all the neediness and desperation you're sure to be feeling. Your message may be "I love you, I can't live without you, take care of me, I'm falling apart, please come back."

Of course your partner needs to hear your authentic pain and vulnerability, but once you've shared them, it won't help to repeat yourself. If you stay stuck in pursuit mode, your partner is likely to become even more allergic to your presence. If you want to win your partner back, or at least give yourself the best chance of saving your marriage, you need to change course. Here's how.

Review the rules for pursuers in chapter 4. I can't overemphasize how much courage and will it takes for a pursuer to stop pursuing. Get all the support you need from family and friends—and *not* from your partner. You may want to start counseling so that you have an additional place to voice your pain and get support. Nothing is more important than taking care of yourself at this time and getting a grip on overwhelming emotions.

Second, gather the courage and willpower to respect your partner's wish for space. Don't plead with her, even if you have to win an Academy Award trying to act like a pulled-together, mature person who is dedicated to moving forward in his life. If you're too emotional to do this in person, write a handwritten note.

Here's an example from a therapy client of mine:

> *Dear Jill,*
>
> *I apologize for being on your back and not respecting your need for space. I feel like I've turned a corner. I've started therapy and I'm getting the help I need. This crisis has forced me to take a good, hard look at myself and my contribution to the problems in our marriage. I realize that I need to focus on my own issues at this time. I support whatever you need to do for yourself, and I want you to know that I'm going to be okay and that I'm taking good care of myself. I love you and I hope we can make the marriage work. Whenever you're ready to talk, let me know.*
>
> *Love, Tim*

Before Tim sent this card (not an e-mail!), he was leaving several messages a day on Jill's machine, sending her long e-mails, and asking friends to intervene on his behalf. He expressed an urgent need to "fight like hell to win Jill back" and told me that if only she'd talk to him, he knew he could convince her to stay. But it was this letter, and Tim's dedication to working on himself, that ultimately caught Jill's attention. She began to remember all that was good in the marriage and to rethink her decision to divorce.

Writing such a letter may feel utterly false, but this is creative pretending at its best. Later Tim got in touch with the higher truth in the letter. He *did* need to work on himself. Jill *did* need space. He *was* going to be okay, even though it sure didn't feel that way to him at the time.

It takes a huge amount of discipline to say less when you feel compelled to say more, to not pursue when you feel desperate to do so, to turn your attention to your own issues, and to let your partner know you are moving forward. To follow this rule, you'll need to swim hard against the emotional tide, because nothing leaves us more vulnerable than the threat of relationship loss. The payoff for trying to follow this rule is that it will put you on the firmest possible footing, whether or not you're able to rescue your marriage.

NINE

HELP YOUR MARRIAGE SURVIVE STEPKIDS

Ever feel there should be a medal of honor for hanging on to your marriage while raising stepkids? Okay, maybe that's stretching it a bit, but making a marriage work with stepchildren at home requires courage, fortitude, and grace under pressure. In fact, it's harder than you can possibly anticipate at the time you decide to couple up when one or both of you just happen to have kids. And let's light a little candle for stepmothers, because the difficulty of their position can't be overstated.

A brief warning about this chapter: While reading it, you may feel that you've just been given a plate of overcooked liver dressed with dry Brussels sprouts. But my purpose in serving it straight up is a worthy one: Marriages with stepchildren have the very best chance to thrive and blossom when the many myths and half-truths that surround them are vigorously challenged. So with that warning, here goes.

When a marriage involves rearing children from a pre-

vious relationship, it challenges everyone in the system. The
potential for competition, jealousy, loyalty conflicts, and
enemies within and between households is sky-high. It's no
surprise that the couple relationship quickly becomes overloaded, even when both partners are doing their very best to
make the new marriage work. Adding to the stress is the fact
that much of the advice and couples counseling out there
assumes that your stepfamily can operate like an original
nuclear family. It can't—or at least, not well. Know this: If
you try to form a stepfamily that models itself on the original
nuclear family, your marriage will be strained beyond belief.
Couples in stepfamilies need a different set of roles and rules
and guidelines to succeed.

To acknowledge the complexities of stepfamily life is
certainly not to suggest that this family form is second-best
to the original nuclear family, or that kids can't thrive. A
well-functioning stepfamily can enrich everyone involved.
Despite the unique challenges for the couple, there are countless, well-functioning, happy, and thriving marriages in stepfamilies. Armed with knowledge, support, and determination
to follow the rules in this chapter, you can make your marriage one of them.

The essence of most of the rules is this: Stepmothers and
stepfathers should do only what's realistic and no more, while
mothers and fathers must step up to the plate and take charge
of their own kids. It goes without saying that things will go
more smoothly if the pain and anger from the dissolution of
a previous marriage have been truly resolved, and if you and

your partner treat all of the adults involved in a child's care with courtesy and respect, even if those other adults are behaving badly. Like most things that are worthwhile, this is easier said than done.

Half of marriages that occur every year are remarriages, and about one out of three children will live with a stepparent at some point. I thank family therapy pioneers Betty Carter and Monica McGoldrick for teaching me about the particular challenges that face couples in remarried families with stepkids. The rules that follow reflect what I've learned from them and want to pass on to you.

Rule #89
FORGET ABOUT BLENDING

Some of my colleagues like the term *"blended family"* ("just add kids and stir"). But here's the problem: Families don't blend. Obviously, life is simpler when stepkids are already launched at the time of a remarriage or are so young that there's lots of time to develop a new history with them. But stepfamily life is rarely simple with kids in the house. It usually takes three to five years for all family members to make some kind of adjustment. Rather than blending, you may be more likely to feel that you and your partner have been put through the blender.

Better to embrace the complexity. When two people marry or couple up for the first time, they bring to their relationship the usual emotional baggage from their family of origin. When you form a stepfamily, one or both of you also carry the emotional baggage from your first marriage and from the painful termination of that marriage through divorce or death. If you're now a stepmother, the whole world will expect you to take care of his children along with any you might have, because this is "what women do." If you're the natural father, you're likely to feel tied in knots from the negativity between your new wife and your child—or between your wife and your ex—and you don't have a clue how to make things better. If you're the stepfather you may try to step into an authority role with your wife's children, only to find that your well-intentioned efforts are rebuffed.

If you have the fantasy that all the children and adults will quickly feel "at home" in your new stepfamily, let it go. Rather than blaming any one person, try to appreciate that you're part of a very complex system and that even a highly evolved Zen Buddhist would have trouble maintaining a calm and clear head on most days. Go slow, be patient, expect intensity, and drop the dream of blending everyone into a family "smoothie."

Rule #90
DON'T PUSH FOR CLOSENESS

Forging a new family takes time. In the early phases of step-family life, both stepmoms and stepdads need to be sensitive to the importance of hanging out on the periphery. For example, if your wife enjoyed a special birthday ritual with her son before your marriage, you might

> Hanging out on the periphery is essential.

encourage her to continue the ritual as usual—just the two of them—rather than insisting that you come along. With time, your family can create new rituals of your own.

If there is a teen in the house, hanging out on the periphery is essential. Teens are especially confused by demands that they bond with their new family because they're trying to separate from the family they already have. So if you've cooked a delicious dinner for the whole family and your husband's two teenage kids opt out to eat with friends, don't take it out on them. And don't blame him for not reading them the riot act. Unless this is a special dinner that everyone is expected to attend, chalk it up to normal teen behavior. Just put the leftovers in the refrigerator for the kids to snack on when they come home, and don't take their last-minute absence personally.

If *his* adolescent daughter is on the scene, she may be her stepmother's greatest challenger. Eldest daughters, especially, tend to be loyal and protective of their mothers, and they may also have enjoyed a special position as caretaker of their divorced dad. If you're stepping into a family that includes his teenage daughter, it's best to reduce your expectations for closeness to that daughter to near zero.

Rule #91

STEPMOTHERS: DON'T TRY TO BE ANY KIND OF MOTHER!

The very term *stepmother* is loaded with false assumptions. The word *step* is derived from the word *orphan,* so right away the label *stepmother* implies something less than optimal, as our time-honored fairy tales illustrate so well. But the real problem with the word *stepmother* is the *"mother"* part.

Women marry because they've fallen in love with a guy, and not because they're necessarily looking to be anybody's mother. Most important, nobody can walk into a family that has a history of its own and become an instant mother. The role of mother—any kind of mother—cannot be automatically conferred on a woman when she marries a man with children.

It will help your marriage if you recognize the absurdity of such an expectation and the problems it creates. The harder the new wife tries to become some kind of mother, the more resistance she'll get from her stepchildren and their actual mother. The man's natural tendency to fade into the woodwork will be amplified, especially if he's working harder to support two families. The ground is fertile for mother and stepmother to blame each other.

Meanwhile, the child is caught between two women who are parenting with a hostile edge, and the stepmother provides an on-site target for a distressed child who is acting up. Dad, for his part, may feel like he's caught in the cross fire and is helpless to make things better. The marriage is suffering, which no one anticipated because everyone got along splendidly together before a girlfriend became a new wife and thus a stepmom.

Keep in mind that children rarely voice a wish for another parent. They aren't looking for another mother or father. When asked what kind of relationship they'd like with their parent's new husband or wife, kids express a wish for a friendly relationship of some sort—say, like an aunt or uncle, basketball coach or special pal. No one ever replaces a parent, not even a dead or absent parent, or one who is in jail on charges of grand larceny.

Rule #92
CHALLENGE THOSE TRADITIONAL GENDER ROLES!

Take this as fact: The old gender expectations lurk at the heart of most stepfamily problems. Even in the most modern and egalitarian of couples, these expectations can be quietly sleeping in the bushes, only to leap out five minutes after the remarried couple settles under one roof. If you want to strengthen your marriage, you need to challenge them.

When a typical heterosexual couple is about to retie the knot, family therapist Betty Carter reminds us that they are both likely to be thinking along the following lines.

He says to himself, "Great! I'm getting married again! My kids will have a mother now, and we'll be a real family again!" (Translation: "I'll go to work, she'll raise my kids, and we'll look like a traditional nuclear family again.") Or, worse, he says to himself, "Great! My kids will have a good mother now, who will do a much better job raising them than that selfish, neglectful bitch I'm divorced from."

She says to herself, "Great, I'm getting married again! Now I'll have someone to support me and the kids, since we can hardly make it on the child support I get from their father. I'll raise his girls, since his work keeps him so busy and my schedule is flexible. Plus, he obviously doesn't have a clue about disciplining them. And the poor little darlings never had a mother who put them first, so if I just try hard enough, I can give them what they really need."

These grizzled old gender expectations can be a disaster for your marriage. How can you push against them? First, Dad can discipline his own kids and assume the daily, hands-on job of parenting even when it seems simpler for his wife to do so. Men should know that turning parenting responsibilities over to the new wife will place her in the "wicked stepmother" role and cause his kids to act up. Second, Mom can contribute to income production even though her earning power may be far less than his. This may be good advice for nuclear families too, but the old roles exact the highest price for stepfamilies and ultimately for the marriage.

Even seasoned therapists can slip into taking the traditional path of thinking the man can't be expected to do the primary parenting if his wife is the one on the scene. I recall seeing a couple that was having family problems partly because the husband's business took him out of town on weekdays. His wife of about a year was left to take charge of his three boys (her stepchildren), who always acted up around bedtime.

When the husband insisted that he couldn't possibly take charge of bedtime because he was away so much, I found myself reflexively nodding in agreement. Suddenly I recalled a comment I'd heard Betty Carter make to a father in a similar situation nearly a decade earlier. In her disarming way, she'd asked, "Have you ever heard of the telephone?"

Jarred awake by this memory, I put the dad in charge of calling his boys every night he was on the road. His job was to find out how their day at school went, to let them know his expectations about bedtime, and to insist that they treat their stepmother with respect and good manners when she reminded them it was time to go to bed. All family relationships, and especially their marriage, improved remarkably when he rose to the occasion.

Rule #93

STEPDADS: COACH FROM BEHIND THE SCENES!

Let's face it: Being a stepdad is no walk in the park. If you want to be a positive force in your marriage, be kind and responsible with your stepchildren and show interest in their activities and projects. If they're up for spending one-on-one time with you, go for it. But understand that you can't step into an authority role with your wife's children, no matter how loving you are to them, and no matter how stellar your leadership skills. Parental authority is something to be earned slowly, over time. Aim to be a supportive husband and behind-the-scenes coach around parenting problems—if and when your wife wants coaching. It's key to making *this* marriage last.

Believe in your wife's capacity to raise her children in a way that works for her. Of course, she may be struggling to find her way with discipline for little Jonny, but bite your tongue and stay on the sidelines. If, for example, your wife asks Jonny to set the table and he stays glued to the television, it's not helpful to jump in with "Jonny, did you hear what your mother said? She said come here and set the table! If you have a positive suggestion, tell your wife later in a respectful way. Likewise, don't be a critic. Avoid saying things to your wife like "I can't stand watching how your daughter treats you!" or saying to your stepdaughter "I can't stand listening to you smart-mouth your mother!" Such comments (even if your wife makes them herself, which she

may) can undermine your partner's confidence and competence as a mother, and will ultimately strain the marriage.

Advice to moms: Trust yourself to raise your own children, even if you've married a wonderful man who has always
wanted to be a father and you're convinced that your children will benefit by his assuming some of the discipline
because he's better at it than you are. Don't surrender your
authority, even if you've had nothing but Bad Mother days
since your remarriage. If you're in the middle of a screaming
battle with your twelve-year-old son, it may be tempting to
throw up your hands and yell to your partner "I can't deal
with this anymore! Get in here and take over!" Resist this
impulse and handle the situation yourself, even if you're at a
total loss, as parents often are.

Encourage your husband to leave the room if he can't
stand witnessing the interaction between you and your child.
Let him know that you value his feedback, if it's out of earshot from the kids, and if it's presented respectfully. In sum,
be open to your husband's feelings and good ideas while
holding tight to your ultimate authority as the parent. Support his important role as behind-the-scenes coach. Doing so
will help your kids and can literally save your marriage.

A postscript to stepfathers and stepmothers—if you want to
make your marriage work, keep this paradox in mind: If
you're lucky and you take it slow, you may be able to work

out an emotionally close relationship with your stepchildren. It's certainly possible to develop a parentlike relationship over time if you enter the system when a child is young and you have time to develop a positive history. But you can't command it. Paradoxically, arriving at a parentlike relationship is most likely to happen if you consider it "an extra" and not something you expect and deserve.

> Arriving at a parentlike relationship is most likely to happen if you consider it "an extra" and not something you expect and deserve.

What should be expected is that stepparents and stepchildren treat each other with courtesy and respect. *It's the parent, not the stepparent, who has the primary responsibility to see that this particular expectation is enforced.* When the parent steps up to the plate on this one, it takes a big strain off the marriage.

Rule #94
DON'T ASK "WHO DO YOU LOVE MORE?"

It's a good bet that you and your partner aren't getting enough time alone together, given the needs of kids and the relational challenges everyone is facing. If you're the stepparent, it's normal to feel resentful that you have so little time with your partner that doesn't revolve around a kid or some family problem. It's easy to feel frustrated that he or she isn't available enough. At some point, you may be tempted to ask your partner "Who do you love more, me or your son Billy?"

In stepfamilies, the parent-child bond long predates the new couple bond. Kids come first, and it's normal to feel jealous. But the question "Who do you love more?" is unfair. The particular kind of love and responsibility a parent feels toward a child simply can't be compared to what one feels for a partner. You probably know this, but the chronic stress of family life doesn't bring out the most mature responses in any of us.

Do request alone time with your partner, just as you need to do in an original nuclear family. Marriage expert Bill Doherty suggests a number of rituals to maintain a strong marriage, and one is to spend just fifteen minutes a day together as a couple—no kids, no talk of chores, no nagging. This is a good rule for any family form, because couples today are chronically tired and overextended. The point is to request time without measuring it against the time and attention that your partner gives to his or her child.

Rule #95
CHANGE YOUR STEPS IN THE STEPFAMILY DANCE

Consider this abbreviated stepfamily story as a model for how stepfamilies typically get in—and out—of trouble, irrespective of whether they are straight or gay.

When Amy was dating Victoria, everything bubbled along beautifully. They each had their separate living arrangements, and Victoria got along fine with Amy's ten-year-old son, Jake, who was affectionate and warm toward her.

Amy (the youngest in her family of origin) was a free-spirited mother who acted spontaneously, rarely planning ahead. For example, she'd be driving Jake home at dinnertime and suddenly remember there was no food in the house. They'd pick up pizza or hamburgers and coke at the drive-through and eat dinner in front of the television, having a contest over who could belch more loudly. Like many youngests, Amy sometimes acted more like a peer than a parent. But Amy and Jake adored each other, and although Amy sometimes expressed insecurity about her parenting, she and Jake were doing just fine.

Victoria, a firstborn in her family of origin, was a highly organized person who was five years Amy's senior. She had launched a daughter of her own from a previous marriage. It wasn't until Amy and Victoria had a commitment ceremony, and Victoria moved into Amy's house, that Victoria discovered she couldn't tolerate Amy's "looseness" when it came to parenting and household organization.

Victoria met only token resistance from Amy when she began to impose her own rules on the household. Fast food was out, as was eating in front of the television. Jake was to make his bed every morning and was allowed to watch a maximum of seven hours of television a week.

The more Victoria moved toward the emotional center of the family, the more Jake rejected her. Who was this new adult who was dramatically altering his relationship with his mom—whom, by the way, he no longer had to himself? Worst of all, this new person was acting like she was a better mother than his real one, and his real mother was no longer behaving like much of a mother, which Jake experienced as an abandonment.

When I saw the couple in therapy, their relationship was a mess. Jake's grades had dropped sharply, from mostly A's to mostly C's. Amy, caught in the middle of angry struggles between Jake and Victoria, was depressed and terrified that Victoria would leave her. Victoria, meanwhile, was close to giving up. She had moved in full of hope and positive expectations, and now she felt overwhelmed, unappreciated, and pretty thoroughly fed up with Jake.

What to do? Recognizing that the survival of their relationship was at stake, to say nothing of their sanity, both women began to rise to the occasion. Amy once again took charge of raising her son. Out of respect for Victoria, she learned to run a tighter ship, setting new rules for Jake and

SURVIVE STEPKIDS227

enforcing them ("You can keep your bedroom a mess, but not the public space").

Victoria had the incredibly difficult job of moving to the periphery and leaving Amy the space to struggle to bring more order and structure into Jake's life. Amy had to learn to assert and reassert her authority as Jake's mother whenever Victoria moved from giving helpful feedback to being outright controlling. With practice, Amy learned to say "Victoria, you have wonderful ideas about parenting, and I want to hear them. But it's not helpful when you get judgmental or tell me what to do. And there are some things we simply see differently. I need to raise Jake in a way that makes sense to me, even if I make mistakes."

When the threesome became a stepfamily, Amy did a great job of telling Jake "Victoria will never replace your dad." The part she left out was "Victoria will never replace *me*." Remember that kids need to hear *both* messages if they are going to accept a new adult on the scene.

Rule #96

SUPPORT KIDS' CONNECTIONS IN BOTH HOUSEHOLDS AS A SPIRITUAL PRACTICE

If you want your marriage and stepfamily to grow stronger, support the children's relationships with everyone in the other household. If you can't imagine feeling positively toward some other adult in the system, pretend kindness and respect. Consider it your spiritual practice.

This means that if your fifteen-year-old stepdaughter, Anna, comes home and reports that her mother says you're a control freak, you need to *under*react. Don't criticize back. If you add fuel to the fire, family relationships will intensify and your marriage will ultimately suffer.

Sure, it may be tempting to say "Well, Anna, your mother thinks I'm controlling because she's a loose cannon" or "Your mother just doesn't like me and never will." Or "I think your mother is threatened and wants to turn you against me." Maybe you say nothing but your stepdaughter can see that you're seething. Or you act sad and wounded, and withdraw from the conversation. Maybe you confront your husband with how pissed off you are. You may insist he call his wife that very evening and tell her to stop poisoning your relationship with Anna with her crazy lies.

> Take the high road. It's hard. And it's worth it.

Try mightily to avoid all of the above. Instead, let it go. Take some deep breaths and remind yourself that it is totally normal for your stepdaughter's mother to be anxious and threatened by your position in the family. Underreacting means you don't take the bait and you don't intensify the triangle further.

Instead you might laugh and say "Well, I may be a bit of a control freak. I'm probably not as spontaneous and free as your mom is." Or "Well, your mom and I are two different people, and it makes sense that we have pretty different styles." Or, if Anna quotes her mother as saying you're some kind of dangerous weirdo, "You know, I see that differently from your mom. I really don't recognize myself in that picture."

It makes an enormous difference if you can say these things in a low-key way, with no edge in your voice. Nothing is more important than learning to transmit less intensity than you receive. Lightness and humor tend to loosen up triangles, while intensity only makes them more rigid.

Keep in mind that the primary concern of children is how their actual parents are treating them and how the grown-ups on both sides are treating each other. They don't want you to circle the wagons around your stepfamily or do anything to threaten their ties with aunts, uncles, cousins, and grandparents on the "other side." More than anything, they don't want a negative or critical focus among any of the adults involved in their care.

Keep trying to support your stepkids' relationships with *all* family members. Ditto for supporting your own child's relationship with your ex and his family. This is a position of integrity that over time will strengthen your marriage. Try to view the obnoxious behaviors of adults on the "other side" as nothing more than a barometer of their anxiety level and their immature way of managing it. Take the high road. It's hard. And it's worth it.

TEN

YOUR FIRST FAMILY: THE ROYAL ROAD TO A REMARKABLE MARRIAGE

Long before we are partners in marriage, we are sons and daughters, sisters and brothers. Our first family is the most influential system we ever belong to, and it provides us with our first blueprint of what marriage looks like. It's also the laboratory in which we learn to speak up (or not), negotiate and compromise (or not), manage conflict and differences (or not), and relate to each other honestly and respectfully (or not).

As children, we were largely powerless to question the family party line or challenge the roles that we and others played out. Children—by virtue of their utter economic and emotional dependence—learn to silence parts of themselves in order to belong. But now, as adults who are trying to figure out our own marriages, it's up to us to decide how we will conduct all of our relationships, including those with the folks who shaped us way back when. How we relate to our first family after we marry will have a profound effect on the marriage itself.

Contrary to conventional wisdom, you can't achieve independence by moving out of your parents' home, landing a paying job, and renting an apartment with your partner halfway across the country. Rather, true independence requires the following: You can stay connected to family members while remaining yourself. You can say what you think and feel without trying to change or convince the other person, and without getting defensive or attacking. You can ask questions about family history and get a more objective, three-dimensional picture of family members. You can observe and change your part in dysfunctional family patterns. This business of maintaining both the "I" and the "we"—and not losing either when the going gets rough—is the largest of all human challenges. Working on it in your first family is the royal road to a better marriage.

You may not want to hear that your family of origin exerts such a powerful influence on your couple relationship. You might even have thought of marriage as a way of freeing yourself from the influence of these dysfunctional folks. Sorry, it doesn't work that way. But there's good news too. You can improve your marriage without working directly on it! Follow the rules in this chapter and you'll stand on more solid ground with your partner, and you'll be able to navigate even the most difficult issues with greater creativity and less reactivity. It's ultimately more work not to establish healthy patterns with your first family. Take my word for it—or better yet, be a bold adventurer and do the research yourself!

Rule #97

BE A GOOD CITIZEN IN YOUR FAMILY OF ORIGIN

Marriage gets overloaded when it's all the family we have. This is one of many reasons to be responsibly connected to your first family. Aim to be a good citizen in your family—including the extended family—just like you'd aim to be a member in good standing in any organization in which you wanted to be valued and heard. You'll also model a commitment to family for your partner and children if you have them, helping to make good citizenship a tradition across generations.

Good citizenship requires these four things:

1. *Show up at important family events.* Try to be present for the major life cycle events. These include graduations, bar or bat mitzvahs or Quinceañeras, weddings, family reunions, key birthdays, and funerals. When you can't show up, figure out the next best way to connect. Pick up the phone, send flowers or cards, or do whatever reflects the values and tastes of the person and event you are recognizing. Participate in family events and rituals even when it feels like a chore.

2. *Don't allow your partner to define your relationships to your own family.* No matter how hard your partner makes it for you to stay connected

to your family, the responsibility is 100 percent yours. Of course, if you move your cousin Jack into the basement without having negotiated this with your partner, then it becomes very much her business. Ditto if your mother is rude to your partner and you can't find a kind way to talk to her about it. Your relationship with a family member should never be at your partner's expense—and vice versa.

3. *Connect with several functional relatives on your family tree.* If you look at any family over several generations, you'll see saints and sinners, good guys and bad guys. If you think your little nuclear family is a hotbed of pathology, make it a special point to find the more functional relatives in your extended family and get to know them a bit. These people are also your family. The more connections you make, the more objective you'll be able to be about your family, yourself, and ultimately your marriage.

4. *Formulate your own beliefs about "good citizenship."* Take the time to reflect on your own values. What do you think it means to be a good son, daughter, parent, grandparent, aunt, uncle, or cousin? Act from your core values and beliefs, and not simply in reaction to the less-than-responsible actions of other family members.

A note for this rule and those that follow: It's a good idea to maintain some contact witheven the most difficult family members. But if the idea of contact fills you with dread, and you can't manage the anxiety, your first priority

> No matter how hard your partner makes it for you to stay connected to your family, the responsibility is 100 percent yours.

is protecting yourself. If you know you need to keep your distance, do so.

Rule #98

GET THE BIG PICTURE: DRAW A FAMILY TREE!

Remember the old adage "What you don't know won't hurt you"? Well, research on families doesn't support that one. The less you know about your family history, the more likely you are to repeat family patterns or mindlessly rebel against them. Nor can you know your parents as real people without rooting them—and yourself—in the factual history of your family, for as far back as you can gather the data.

Perhaps you're convinced that you already know your family. Most of us have stories we like to tell about family members—and maybe a psychiatric diagnosis to throw in as well ("My mother has a narcissistic personality disorder"). The stories we tell over and over may elicit other people's admiration ("Your brother sounds like an incredible person!") or their sympathy ("I can't believe that your father was so rigid and critical!"). We get stuck in these stories and don't want them disrupted by facts.

Go for the facts while family members are still alive to provide them. Talk to your parents if you can, and eventually to other living relatives. And I mean talk, the old-fashioned, face-to-face way, or, failing that, by telephone. Don't wait until everyone is dead before wondering how old your mother was when her mother died or where your ancestors came from. Don't rely on the many pages of names and dates that your cousin Sam has gathered from his extensive genealogical research, because nothing can replace connecting with family members and opening up the conversations yourself. Draw your own family tree.

Like all things worth doing, gathering family history is a long-term project, usually done in fits and starts. If you stay with it over time, you'll find that asking questions elicits new stories, which then evoke more questions on your part. You'll also learn the hot spots in your history by paying attention to what family members don't want to talk about, and what you're not comfortable asking about. Chances are, the hot spots in your family will show up in your marriage.

Mapping out the history of your family on paper will give you a richer view of the story in which your own marriage is a chapter. And knowing your partner's family history will tune you in to the particular challenges and vulnerabilities she or he inherited along with hair color and height.

Rule #99
BECOME A BRILLIANT QUESTIONER

When Isidor I. Rabi, Nobel Laureate in physics, was once asked what motivated him to become a scientist, he credited his Jewish mother from Brooklyn. He explained that all the other mothers would ask their children after school if they had learned anything. But his mother always asked something else. "Izzy," she would say, "did you ask a good question today?"

"That difference—asking good questions—made me a scientist," Rabi said.

Become a scientist in your own family. Learn to ask good questions and to listen well. Asking questions will allow you to know your parents as real people, who had a personal history of their own long before you entered the picture. The more you can see your parents objectively, the more you will see yourself and your partner objectively. And if you can ask questions about sensitive subjects in your family history, you'll carry less underground intensity and anxiety into your marriage. Here are a few things to keep in mind.

Start slowly, by calmly asking for basic facts before you jump into high-twitch areas. To start inquiring about your relatives, you might say "The older I get, the more I realize that I don't know very much about my family. I started doing a family tree and wonder if you can help me fill in some names and dates." Aim to be both curious and respectful when inquiring about your family.

If you're delving deeper, ask questions that are specific. Parents often feel at a loss with global questions like "How did you feel about your dad dying so young?" or "What was your relationship like with your mother?" Instead, try to ask very well-defined questions: "After your dad died, did you become closer or more distant with your mom?" "Who in the family came to the funeral?" "Did your mom talk about her feelings and her grief, or was she more a stoic sort of person?" Parents and other family members are often surprisingly forthcoming with information if they know it will be helpful to you, and if they trust that they're not going to be criticized, blamed, or diagnosed.

> If you can ask questions about sensitive subjects in your family history, you'll carry less underground anxiety into your marriage.

Don't overload the circuits: Gather a little information at a time. As you talk, be aware of the other person's emotions, and draw the session to a close before a parent or other relative becomes tired or overwhelmed. Important conversations don't require a marathon meeting. Revisit issues and ask questions over time.

Rule #100
SPEAK TO THE DIFFERENCES!

Learning to *speak to the differences* with family members is one of the most growth-fostering exercises you can practice to strengthen your relationship. In fact, you may not be able to make yourself heard with your partner until *after* you can say to your mother (and father, sister, uncle) "You know, Mom, I see it differently. Let me tell you how I see it."

What does it mean to "speak to the differences"? It's not about confronting a family member, which is rarely a growth-enhancing move. When we head into a confrontation, we're out to change or convince the other person, which isn't possible. We may secretly want to make the other person feel as bad as they've made us feel, which also won't happen and won't help.

In contrast, speaking to the differences means that we can calmly share our thoughts and feelings, and allow the other person to do the same, without getting too nervous about differences and without having to fix or shape up the other party. Far from letting the other person off the hook, practicing this rule invites the other person to sit in the hot seat and tolerate some discomfort.

Joanna, a therapy client who was married to Carolina, was on the receiving end of homophobic comments from her mother, who treated Joanna's marriage to a woman as a problem to be tolerated. Joanna would snap at her mother, try to educate her, or seethe silently—none of which was productive. The breakthrough came when Joanna spoke calmly to their differences and simply asked her mother to reflect on the matter. "Mom," she said, "I have the impression from our talks that you think being gay is a problem I was born with and that you should accept it because you love me. I have a different perspective. When I first became aware of my feelings for women, I was scared and wondered what was wrong with me, but that's changed totally over time. My marriage to Carolina is the best thing that's ever happened to me, and even if she weren't in the picture, I wouldn't choose to change who I am or become straight. What's it like for you that we see this so differently?"

Joanna's mother rose to the occasion and shifted gears as she tried to honor Joanna's marriage rather than simply tolerating it. But even if she had responded badly, Joanna had found her adult voice. In this conversation and others, Joanna expressed pride in who she was, and she affirmed the new family that she and Carolina had established. She did this without getting defensive or attacking, and without needing to change or convince her mother.

Every family has high twitch-areas where it can be quite challenging to say "You know, Mom, I see it differently. Let me tell you how I see it." If you stay on course with your first family, you will build a more solid self and be more able to find your own voice with your partner as well.

Rule #101
DON'T LET FAMILY VISITS HIJACK YOUR MARRIAGE

When we couple up, we face the challenge of maintaining a healthy boundary between the new family we've created and the two families we come from. If family visits have been stressful in the past, be thoughtful about managing them in the future. Follow these steps.

1. *Don't leave it to your partner to plan for the visit or entertain your family.* If your family visits you from out of town, take a day or two off work. If this is truly impossible, leaving work a few hours earlier on a particular day will signal to a family member that they matter. Go out of your way to be present during the visit.

2. *Connect one-on-one.* Invite each family member to do something one-on-one with you, even if it's a ten-minute walk around the block with your mom or a quick coffee at the local coffee shop with your brother, where you just banter about sports and the weather.

3. *Structure the length of visits.* Obviously this may require compromise. It's not reasonable, for example, to tell your parents who are flying in to see you from Japan that they can only stay for a long weekend. That said, stay in charge of the

length of visits. If your family is like many, things can get too intense after about four or five days (if not four or five minutes). When it comes to family visits, longer is not necessarily better.

4. *Get space.* Take breaks when you need them during visits, which can include everything from leaving the house for a brisk walk, to planning a three-day mini-trip with your partner within a ten-day visit to your parents. If visiting family has been extremely difficult for you or your partner, spring for a hotel and rental car. This can make the difference between a good-enough visit and a disaster, so these are dollars well spent. Your parents may be insulted you're not staying in the guest room, but they'll get over it in subsequent visits if you use your creativity to provide a tactful explanation.

> Springing for a hotel and rental car can make the difference between a good-enough visit and a disaster.

5. *Anticipate the hot spots.* You know your family well enough to know what will make you clutch and react. It may be your sister's comments on your son's "wild" behavior, your mother's relentless focus on your brother's screwups, or your

father talking about his business schemes. Make a plan to manage the conversation and your own reactivity so things don't escalate. Tell your partner how he or she can help you.

6. *Set reasonable goals.* Survival is a perfectly reasonable goal for a family visit if you come from a family where intensity and reactivity runs high. Observing your family is another worthwhile goal. Getting through a visit without participating in any fights is another. If you feel up to the challenge, set the bar higher and experiment with new behaviors, such as refraining from advice giving, asking your dad to take a walk with you, eliciting family stories, sharing a personal problem, or trying the 5:1 ratio of positive to negative comments with your mom.

Marriage includes the challenge of managing contact with family in mature and thoughtful ways. The challenge is to think ahead and plan—rather than react emotionally and take the stress out on an innocent party—your partner.

Rule #102

SUPPORT YOUR PARTNER 100 PERCENT WITH HER FAMILY

Your partner's family is not just her problem—or blessing. In a successful relationship, partners can rely on each other for support with family members. Here are five ways to support your partner with her family, whether you feel like it or not. Every bit of support you give her will strengthen the bond between you and earn your partner's admiration and gratitude over time.

1. *Support your partner's close family ties.* If your partner is extremely tight with her sister, learn to appreciate, or at least tolerate, the fact that she wants to spend lots of time with her on family visits or talk at great length on the phone. It's normal to feel jealous of this lifelong bond that predates your relationship, but aim for generosity of spirit. Instead of acting grumpy and abandoned, try saying something like "I'm happy to watch the kids so you and your sister can go out together."

2. *Honor the culture of her family.* If your partner's family loves board games, or family reunions in Branson, Missouri, be a good sport even if you'd prefer to be museum hopping in Manhattan.

Join in enthusiastically even though it's not your thing. Your role during her family visits is to support your partner while building your own relationships with your in-laws.

3. *Help your partner with difficult family members.* Invite her most difficult family member to spend an afternoon with you during a visit. Not only will this give your partner a breather but you'll also get to know her family better, which means knowing your partner better too. Offer to get on the phone with her when she makes an annual birthday call to a difficult aunt. Since you don't have a childhood history with your partner's family, it will be easier for you to step in, no matter how unpleasant you find the task.

4. *Be a listener, not an instigator.* If your partner has a family member neither of you can stand, it's important to support your spouse without fanning the flames of her anger. Your partner needs to vent without being given more reasons to be upset. Often the best thing we can do is say "I really understand why that's so upsetting, and I'm here for you to help however I can." What's not helpful is "You're right, Fred *is* the worst brother in the world! Remember that time he showed up two hours late to your birthday dinner?"

5. *Ask your partner how you can be helpful.* This doesn't mean you agree to drive the car into the river with her nagging parents in the backseat. But you can use humor, distraction, and love to help her get calmer. Be empathetic when her situation is harder than yours: "My family is so easy to deal with that I can't begin to imagine what it's like to have to deal with such a difficult father."

Supporting your partner doesn't mean joining your partner in her angry intensity toward a family member, or having an "anything goes" policy. It means encouraging her to maintain family connections while supporting her best thinking—and doing your own best thinking while you're at it.

Rule #103
AVOID CUTOFFS

There's no such thing as a "clean break" with our family of origin. Here's the paradox: When we cut off from a significant family member, it actually makes them a more dramatic presence in our life. We carry that person around all the time without even knowing it. When we sever a connection that is part of our family history, the feelings we're avoiding don't go away. Instead they go underground and pop up in our relationship with our partner, and often with children if we have them. Cutoffs from our family of origin, including extended family, do not help our marriage.

Cutoffs are an extreme form of distancing, where we try to lower our intensity by erasing family members from our lives as if they no longer exist. People don't cut off lightly or because they are mean or unfeeling. To the contrary, people cut off to protect themselves from potentially unmanageable emotions and to try to get comfortable. In my father's family, where there was a fair degree of trauma, cutoffs were everywhere on his family tree. His mother was cut off from every single person in her family of origin, and also from her only daughter, my aunt Ann, who then cut off from both my sister

> When we cut off from a significant family member we carry that person around all the time.

and me. This was a legacy I became determined *not* to follow and pass down to the next generation.

Respect whatever need for distance you have at present. Also try to envision a future that is not set in stone. Something may shift that allows you to consider a safe way to manage some form of contact. You will be a tad bit lighter with your partner if you can consider the possibility that one day you may find a safe way to reconnect with someone who is part of your history—and therefore part of you and what you bring to your marriage.

Rule #104
SPEAK UP—DON'T STEW

You probably have at least one family member you'd like to turn in at *The Family Exchange Store*. If you are an extremely mature person, you'll recognize that this person's judgmental, intrusive, rude, or otherwise obnoxious behavior is about her (or him) and not about you, and that furthermore this same family member has good intentions and is simply acting out insecurity or unhappiness. But since we're wired for reactivity—and family doesn't bring out the maturity in anybody—it's more likely you may be stewing about someone's upsetting behavior, particularly if it's habitual. If this is the case, it's better for your mental and marital health to speak up—once you've calmed down, of course.

You might say "I respect that you would parent differently (or eat differently, or decorate differently, or organize the kitchen differently), but this is how we do it in this house." You might ask a question that invites accountability: "Mom, are you proud of our daughter, Molly? From the way you talk about Aaron (her other grandchild), I sometimes get the feeling that he's way up here in your eyes, and that Molly is down here." You might make a direct request: "Dad, when you make comments about Mom, I feel uncomfortable. I need to have a relationship with both of you, and I'd prefer you don't talk about Mom when you're with me."

Because automatic behaviors are difficult to change, you may need to sound like a broken record, and also come to terms with the fact that another family member may never get a grip, no matter how well you communicate and no matter how much they love you. Still, it's important to speak up.

Take great care how you communicate. Striking back in anger, or even with an edge in your voice, won't help. Parents in particular tend to be defensive and vulnerable and will shut down in a second if you say something that flips them into the experience of being a bad mother or bad father. Keep in mind that family relationships are more difficult to repair than the one you have with your partner. If you erupt in anger at your spouse on a bad day, the dailiness of living together and the primacy of the relationship provide opportunities to patch up a fight or simply move on. It's far more difficult to repair a broken connection with a family member, especially one who doesn't live nearby. So when you speak up, do so wisely and well.

Rule #105
IN-LAWS: KNOW WHO'S RESPONSIBLE FOR WHAT!

When one partner (usually the man) *under*deals with a parent or family member, the other partner (usually the woman) is likely to *over*deal with that same person. One common outcome is the "mother-in-law triangle," where the man keeps a cordial distance from his mother and avoids speaking up to her when appropriate. The negative intensity then lands between the wife and mother-in-law. The solution: Step to the plate with your own mother. Don't leave it to your partner to be the emotional reactor.

Jack came to see me at a crisis point, desperate because his wife and his widowed mother, Rosa, couldn't get along. Things reached a fever pitch when Rosa, who lived in California, visited them in Kansas City and hit the ground running, criticizing Judy's mothering—from how she fed the kids (not enough protein) to her failure to give them sufficient responsibilities ("They don't even have to clear the table!"). In response, Judy told Jack that she'd had enough and that his mother could never visit again. Jack tried to "explain" his mother to Judy, which only strengthened Judy's resolve that her mother-in-law would never step foot in their house.

I helped Jack speak up to both his wife and his mother. First, he told Judy he would not bar his mother from visiting. He stood by this bottom-line position in a loving and firm way. No one should ever have to choose between a parent and a spouse. Jack also apologized to Judy for handing her the responsibility of entertaining his mother when she visited. "I'm sorry that I haven't talked with Mom about her criticism of you," he said. "I know she gets on you a lot, and it's not okay." He let Judy know that he would be opening up this conversation with his mother.

Jack then had to walk his talk. He took a day off from work and made sure he had alone time with his mother. He asked Rosa how she was *really* doing and shared a problem he was having at work, rather than keeping things cordial and superficial. This in itself eased things up, because Rosa's critical stance toward Judy had everything to do with the fact that she felt she had lost Jack after he'd married. Indeed, the frequency of his phone calls had dropped off dramatically, and when he had called, the conversation had been superficial.

Jack also made a plan to talk to his mother in a loving, non-blaming way about her criticisms of Judy. Jack said, "Mom, you and Judy are the two most important women in my life. Judy is my wife and you're my mother, and I need the two of you to get along and treat each other with respect. I know you're an expert on raising kids and Judy and I are still figuring it out. But even if we make mistakes, we need to do it our own way. And we need your respect and support, even when you don't agree." He made sure his mother knew that Judy's child-rearing practices were as much his as hers.

Jack stood firm when the countermoves started rolling in, and he used humor and tact to stand his ground. When Rosa argued, "I don't criticize Judy, I only want to help. She just doesn't want to hear anything from me!" Jack listened and then said, "Mom, you have so much wisdom about being a mother. You did a great job raising me, which is why Judy fell in love with your son! But right now Judy and I need to make our own mistakes." When his mom replied bitterly, "Well then, I'll keep *all* my opinions to myself," Jack hugged her and said, "Well, Mom, if you believe we need to be doing something differently, I want you to tell *me* about it. You know, Mom, I'm up to hearing whatever you want to suggest."

This shift was not accomplished in one hit-and-run conversation but rather by Jack staying on track over time, and getting back on track after getting derailed. Judy also did her part to dismantle the triangle by learning to underreact to her mother-in-law with lightness and humor. For example, when Rosa told Judy their daughter was wasting away and looked like a twig ever since the family turned vegetarian, Judy joked with her instead of getting hooked. ("Do you really think Emma is going to be as skinny as a twig? Well, we have so many pumpkins on my family tree, we could use a few more twigs.") She also responded to Rosa's good qualities (everyone has some), which gave Jack more emotional space to figure out his relationship with his mother.

The payoff of this work was not simply that Rosa's visits were easier and that Jack developed a real relationship with his mother rather than a superficial one. Jack's self-esteem and confidence were also much enhanced. What Judy didn't anticipate—and at first found a bit stressful—was that she would end up with a husband who was far more outspoken (in the best sense of the word) than the man she had first married. When we find our voice with members of our first family, we automatically bring a stronger, more assertive self to our marriage.

Rule #106
E-MAIL: DO NOT PRESS SEND!

Post this sticky note on your computer: *"If you are feeling angry, misunderstood, or otherwise intense, do not write that e-mail!"* If you're the one on the receiving end of an emotionally loaded e-mail, don't respond in kind. Instead, send a short response that says, "Thanks for your honesty. I'll give what you're saying lots of thought. Let's set up a time to talk on the phone, or when we're next together." Take the exchange off e-mail, and keep it off e-mail.

Most disastrous are long e-mails (even longer than this rule) with all the details you believe will help the other person see the irrefutable truth of your point, or really get the extent of your hurt. I haven't done a large-scale study, but my informal observations suggest that the higher the word count on an emotionally loaded e-mail, the faster the relationship slides downhill.

> *Say* what you want to say—or let it go.

The tone (easily misread) and process of e-mail is very different from a face-to-face conversation. Even a short, constructive criticism on e-mail can lead to escalating intensity. A client of mine, Gennie, was irritated at her younger brother, Joe, who often crashed at her house without lifting a finger to help cook, set or clear the table, or in any way pitch in. After one of his visits, she wrote an e-mail saying, "It was great to have you, but I need to tell you that we're not running a hotel here. Please pitch in and help next time you stay with us." Her brother, whom I imagine had a major shame attack, wrote back a longer, defensive response, which led to an even longer explanatory e-mail from Gennie, which culminated in an e-mail from her brother telling her not to worry, he wouldn't be causing her the trouble of more visits.

The disconnection was eventually repaired, but both parties felt injured. *E-mail, not either of these two good folks, was the culprit.* Things would have gone quite differently if Gennie had said to her brother during the visit, "Hey, Joe, come help me set the table" or "Joe, here's the vacuum. Please do the living room while I'm cooking." If he ignored her, another level of conversation would be in order, like "Hey, Joe, help me understand what's going on here. I've asked you twice to help clear the table, and you've ignored me. What's up?"

Face-to-face conversation requires courage, and e-mail requires none. But it's worth it to take the high road and *say* what you want to say—or let it go. Think of every courageous conversation with family members as a terrific training ground for navigating your marriage with clarity, courage, and joyous conviction.

EPILOGUE

I PROMISE YOU THIS

My husband remarked the other evening that we've had many marriages in our forty-plus years together. I agreed. The couple we were as graduate students in New York City and Berkeley was different from the married people we were in Topeka—especially after we became parents. And we've had a different marriage since our boys have grown up, left home, and married. Over time we've grown up, too, which isn't to say we don't occasionally act like eleven-year-olds.

Personal change, like physical change, is at once dramatic and imperceptible. I couldn't say how many different marriages we've had in our long history together. Maybe seven, the number of different apartments and homes we've lived in? Regardless of how many marriages your marriage contains, I can promise you this: *If you stay together over time, your marriage will change in ways you don't expect and can't predict.*

This fact is neither good nor bad—or rather, it's good *and* bad. Bad news first: If your relationship is going along swimmingly now, don't get lazy, because your life together will take unexpected twists and turns. If your relationship is difficult and disappointing, don't lose hope, because change is all we can count on for sure. Taking the long view—which is what marriage is about—should give us both pause and patience.

My second promise: *If you select ten rules in this book (the ten most relevant and meaningful to you) and follow them over time, you will give your relationship an excellent chance of success.* Keep in mind that even a small, significant change today can put your marriage in a dramatically different place six months from now, let alone five or ten years. If this book is in your hands, I believe you're ready to move forward to protect and improve your marriage. I've never had anyone seek my help because they were determined to keep drifting downstream.

So, consider *Marriage Rules* a kind of basic "go-to-guide" for a solid relationship and a stronger self. Run with the rules that work for you. Ignore the rest. May your marriage—and may you—truly flourish.

ACKNOWLEDGMENTS

I have many people to thank.

Jeffrey Ann Goudie and Emily Kofron continue to dem onstrate the tenacity of love and friendship by sticking with me, book after book, editing drafts on short notice and never failing to improve what they read. Marcia Cebulska provided her playwright perspective and frank personal response to whatever I sent her way. To you three: I can't imagine the writing life without you.

My sons, Matt and Ben, were little kids when I published my first book; how amazing to turn to them for help with this project and to reap the benefits of their generosity and enormous expertise. Thanks also to my spectacular daughters-in-law, Josephine Saltmarsh and Ariana Mangual, for valuable feedback, and for unconditional love and support. And a big hug to my sister (and coauthor of our children's books), Susan Goldhor, for her splendid editing suggestions on many chapters.

Others have responded to my call for help along the way. I'm especially grateful to my friend and colleague Julie Cisz for important conversations, and to Joanie Shoemaker for her thoughtful suggestions. Thanks also to Thomas Fox

Averill, William Doherty, Monica McGoldrick, Leonore
Tiefer, Esther Perel, Caryn Miriam-Goldberg, and Brenda
Kissam. And A Great Big Thanks to Marian Sandmeir for
her enthusiastic support and gifted editorial hand.

My intellectual and emotional debts are too numerous to
mention, beginning with the Menninger Foundation where I
completed my postdoctoral training and later joined the
staff. During my decades as a staff psychologist at Menninger,
I had many fine teachers. I was also blessed from the start
with a wonderful network of long-distance feminist colleagues who supported my work during difficult times and
provided me with a new meaning of intellectual community.
By now, so many important theorists, therapists, and innova-
tors in my field have informed my work that it would be
impossible to begin to name them.

When William (Bill) Shinker, founder and president of
Gotham/Avery signed on to publish *Marriage Rules*, I felt like
I had come home. It was Bill, along with Janet Goldstein,
who published my first book, *The Dance of Anger,* and who
launched and nurtured my career as a writer. Bill has always
represented the heart and soul of publishing at its best. I
thank him for his integrity and vision, and for once promising me a home-cooked gourmet meal, which I still plan to
claim. Bill assigned me to his excellent executive editor Lauren Marino, who pushed me hard when I needed it, but still
gave me the space to go my own way. Cara Bedick, Lauren's
clearheaded, efficient assistant, was also a delight to work

with. Judy Myers did an outstanding job copyediting the final manuscript.

It's difficult to find new ways to thank my agent/manager, Jo-Lynne Worley, who has enhanced and supported my work since we teamed up in the fall of 1990. As ever, I count on her unflappable patience, unwavering competence, and enduring friendship. She has never lost faith in my ability to finish a book.

Finally, my ever-expanding network of family and friends tether me to the earth, while my therapy clients and loyal readers have taught me so much. Without you, there would be no books. I also feel compelled to thank the beautiful, embracing, hilly city of Lawrence, Kansas, which has been home since 2002. What a perfect community in which to live and work.

To Steve, my funny, loving, generous, nurturing, and talented psychologist/musician/filmmaker husband of more than forty years . . . well, thanks for everything. When I think about our life together, I can't believe my good luck.

INDEX

Introduction
IT SHOULDN'T BE THAT COMPLICATED – xi

One
WARM THINGS UP – 1

Rule #1 Respect Differences! – 3
Rule #2 Under Stress, Don't Press – 5
Rule #3 Breathe Now, Speak Later – 7
Rule #4 Remember the 5:1 Ratio – 8
Rule #5 God Is in the Details – 10
Rule #6 You Already Know What to Do – 12
Rule #7 Remember the Sandbox – 14
Rule #8 Fake It for Ten Days – 16
Rule #9 Sweat the Small Stuff – 18
Rule #10 Be the One to Change First – 20

Two

DIAL DOWN THE CRITICISM – 23

Rule #11 Become Fluent in "I" Language – 25

Rule #12 Beware of Pseudo "I" Language! – 27

Rule #13 Criticize Above the Belt – 30

Rule #14 Aim for Accuracy – 32

Rule #15 Talk Less – 33

Rule #16 Strike When the Iron Is Cold – 35

Rule #17 Stay Focused – 37

Rule #18 Surprise Him with Praise – 38

Rule #19 Take the "One-a-Day" Challenge – 40

Rule #20 Cut Back on Advice – 42

Rule #21 Stay Alert for Mixed Messages – 44

Three

OVERCOME YOUR L.D.D. (LISTENING DEFICIT DISORDER) – 47

Rule #22 Don't Just Do Something. Stand There! – 49

Rule #23 Stay Curious: You Don't Really Know How She Feels! – 50

Rule #24 Forget About Being Right – 52

Rule #25 Invite What You Dread – 55

Rule #26 Draw the Line at Insults! – 57

Rule #27 Lower Your Defensiveness: A 12-Step Program – 58

Rule #28 Define Your Differences – 63

Rule #29 Help Your Partner Help You Listen – 64

Rule #30 Set Limits on Listening – 66
Rule #31 Tell Your Partner How You Need Him to
          Listen – 68

Four
CALL OFF THE CHASE: HOW TO CONNECT WITH A DISTANT PARTNER – 71

Rule #32 Identify Your Role in the Dance – 74
Rule #33 Don't Try to Make a Cat into a Dog – 76
Rule #34 Don't Judge the Distancer – 78
Rule #35 Make a Date, Not a Diagnosis – 80
Rule #36 Lower Your Intensity – 83
Rule #37 Try Out a "New You" – 85
Rule #38 Turn Off Your Stupid "Smart Phones" – 86
Rule #39 Pursue Your Goals, Not Your Partner – 88
Rule #40 Heed the Danger Signals – 90
Rule #41 Distancers, Wake Up! – 91

Five
FIGHT FAIR! – 95

Rule #42 Make Your Own Rules – 97
Rule #43 Adopt a Distinguished British Houseguest – 98
Rule #44 Stop It! – 100
Rule #45 Accept the Olive Branch – 102
Rule #46 "Leave Me Alone!" Means "Leave Me
          Alone!" – 104
Rule #47 Honor Your Partner's Vulnerability – 106

Rule #48 Apologize – 108

Rule #49 Don't Demand an Apology – 110

Rule #50 Be Flexible: Change for Your Partner – 112

Rule #51 Don't Threaten Divorce – 114

Rule #52 You Can Lose It!—But Very, Very Sparingly – 115

Rule #53 Beware of the Four Horsemen! – 117

Six

FORGET ABOUT NORMAL SEX – 119

Rule #54 Don't Say "Foreplay" – 121

Rule #55 Be Experimental – 123

Rule #56 Stamp Your Sex Fantasy "Normal" – 126

Rule #57 Don't Judge Your Sex Drive – 128

Rule #58 Don't Wait Till You're "in the Mood" – 130

Rule #59 Raise Your Laundry Consciousness – 131

Rule #60 Women: Tell Your Partner What You Want
          Men: Try Not to Be Defensive – 133

Rule #61 Identify the Pursuer-Distancer Dance in
          Bed – 135

Rule #62 Pursuers, Stop Pursuing! Distancers,
          Stop Distancing! – 137

Rule #63 Never Take Monogamy on Faith – 140

Rule #64 Set Limits – 142

Rule #65 Know When to Close Your Gate – 144

Rule #66 Don't Make Your Partner's Affair a Deal-
          Breaker – 146

Seven

KID SHOCK: KEEP YOUR BEARINGS AFTER CHILDREN ARRIVE –149

Rule #67 Don't Trade Your Partner in for the Baby – 152

Rule #68 "Natural" Parent: Back Off! Clueless Parent:
          Step Up! – 154

Rule #69 Nurture Your Relationship, Not Just Your
          Child – 156

Rule #70 Keep Negotiating "Who Does What?" – 160

Rule #71 Solve the "Cost of Childcare" Dilemma! – 163

Rule #72 Don't Let the Inmates Run the Asylum – 165

Rule #73 Don't Go It Alone – 168

Rule #74 Don't Make Your Partner the
          "Bad Guy" – 171

Rule #75 Be Kind to Your Kin—Especially the
          Grandparents – 174

Rule #76 Don't Obsess About Getting It Right – 176

Rule #77 Remember These Ten Survival Tips – 178

Eight

KNOW YOUR BOTTOM LINE – 181

Rule #78 Start Small – 183

Rule #79 Show Her You Mean It – 186

Rule #80 Do Less – 188

Rule #81 Lighten Up as You Toughen Up – 191

Rule #82 Prepare to Be Tested – 192

Rule #83 Think Before You Leap! – 195

Rule #84 Stand Like an Oak, Bend Like Grass – 197

Rule #85 When to—and When Not to—Talk About
           Divorce – 199

Rule #86 When You Voice the Ultimate, Make Yourself
           Heard – 201

Rule #87 You Can Live Without Your Partner – 204

Rule #88 If Your Partner Is Leaving You, Follow
           This Plan – 206

Nine

HELP YOUR MARRIAGE SURVIVE STEPKIDS – 209

Rule #89 Forget About Blending – 212

Rule #90 Don't Push for Closeness – 214

Rule #91 Stepmothers: Don't Try to Be Any Kind of
           Mother! – 216

Rule #92 Challenge Those Traditional
           Gender Roles! – 218

Rule #93 Stepdads: Coach from Behind the Scenes! – 221

Rule #94 Don't Ask "Who Do You Love More?" – 224

Rule #95 Change Your Steps in the Stepfamily
           Dance – 225

Rule #96 Support Kids' Connections in Both Households
           as a Spiritual Practice – 228

Ten

YOUR FIRST FAMILY: THE ROYAL ROAD TO A REMARKABLE MARRIAGE – 231

Rule #97 Be a Good Citizen in Your Family of Origin – 233

Rule #98 Get the Big Picture: Draw a Family Tree! – 236

Rule #99 Become a Brilliant Questioner – 238

Rule #100 Speak to the Differences! – 240

Rule #101 Don't Let Family Visits Hijack Your Marriage – 242

Rule #102 Support Your Partner 100 Percent with Her Family – 245

Rule #103 Avoid Cutoffs – 248

Rule #104 Speak Up—Don't Stew – 250

Rule #105 In-Laws: Know Who's Responsible for What! – 252

Rule #106 E-mail: Do Not Press Send! – 256

Epilogue

I PROMISE YOU THIS – 259